fat-free

COOKING

michelle hayward

Acknowledgements

To Edward and Tenielle for their encouragement, love and support. Thanks to my mom and dad who are both excellent cooks and who have always been a great inspiration for me. Without the love and support of my family and friends this book would never have been written. My gratitude also goes out to all my clients and students that put these wonderful recipes to the test and encouraged me to put my collection of thoughts, recipes and ideas together. Last, but not least, a special thanks to Joy and Linda from Struik.
MICHELLE HAYWARD

NOTE: Because of the slight risk of salmonella, raw eggs should not be served to the very young, the ill or elderly, or to pregnant women.

First published in the UK in 2001 by New Holland Publishers (UK) Ltd
London • Cape Town • Sydney • Auckland

Garfield House, 86–88 Edgware Road, London W2 2EA, United Kingdom
www.newhollandpublishers.com

80 McKenzie Street, Cape Town 8001, South Africa

Level 1, Unit 4, 14 Aquatic Drive, Frenchs Forest, NSW 2086, Australia

218 Lake Road, Northcote, Auckland, New Zealand

10 9 8 7 6 5 4 3 2 1

Copyright © in published edition: Struik Publishers 2001
Copyright © in text: Michelle Hayward 2001
Copyright © in photographs: Craig Fraser/Struik Image Library 2001

ISBN 1 84330 114 8

Publishing Manager: Linda de Villiers
Editor: Joy Clack
Designer: Beverley Dodd
Photographer: Craig Fraser
Stylist: Abigail Donnelly

Reproduction by Hirt & Carter Cape (Pty) Ltd
Printed and bound by Sing Cheong Printing Company Limited

contents

introduction

Unhealthy eating leads to obesity, which in turn increases the risk of a heart attack, a stroke, cancer and diabetes.

Dietary fat is the biggest culprit when it comes to weight gain, so the focus is to cut back on fat intake. By cutting back on the amount of fat in your diet and by doing regular exercise, you will be working towards a healthier you.

Most of us are aware of the benefits of following a healthy eating plan, but find that healthy foods are tedious and difficult to prepare, and tend to see junk food as the easy alternative. The decision to lead a healthy lifestyle that is fat free is probably the most important step you can make towards creating a healthier body and mind.

Controlling blood sugar through diet and exercise can also help you live a healthier, more energetic life. Sugary foods are high in simple carbohydrates, which are quickly converted into glucose. When you eat a slab of chocolate, it causes the blood-sugar level to rise, giving you a quick energy boost. But your sugar level will drop sharply soon afterwards, making you feel worse.

Snacking on complex carbohydrates, such as whole-wheat bread, grains and vegetables, is good for you because they metabolize more slowly and keep your blood-sugar levels stable for longer.

Cardiovascular exercise at a moderate pace, together with strength training, speeds up your metabolism, which helps burn calories and aids weight loss. It is important to increase your pace as you get progressively fitter.

All of the recipes in this book contain 3 g or less of fat per 100 g, enabling you to eat what you love, but still shed those unwanted kilos.

conversion charts

oven temperatures

very low heat	low heat
100 °C/200 °F	140 °C/275 °F/gas mark 1
110 °C/225 °F	150 °C/300 °F/gas mark 2
120 °C/250 °F	160 °C/325 °F/gas mark 3

moderate heat	high heat
180 °C/350 °F/gas mark 4	220 °C/425 °F/gas mark 7
190 °C/375 °F/gas mark 5	230 °C/450 °F/gas mark 8
200 °C/400 °F/gas mark 6	240 °C/475 °F/gas mark 9

very high heat
260 °C/500 °F

weights (general)

125 g	=	4 oz	=	¼ lb
250 g	=	8 oz	=	½ lb
375 g	=	12 oz	=	¾ lb
448 g	=	16 oz	=	1 lb
1 kg	=	35.2 oz	=	2.2 lb

weights (flour)

30 g	=	60 ml	=	¼ cup
40 g	=	85 ml	=	⅓ cup
60 g	=	125 ml	=	½ cup
120 g	=	250 ml	=	1 cup

measures and equivalents
Note: All measures are taken level.

1 ml	=	a pinch
2 ml	=	¼ teaspoon
3 ml	=	½ teaspoon
5 ml	=	1 teaspoon
7 ml	=	1¼ teaspoons
8 ml	=	1½ teaspoons
10 ml	=	2 teaspoons
20 ml	=	4 teaspoons
15 ml	=	1 tablespoon
30 ml	=	2 tablespoons
45 ml	=	3 tablespoons
60 ml	=	¼ cup
85 ml	=	⅓ cup
125 ml	=	½ cup
165 ml	=	⅔ cup
180 ml	=	¾ cup
250 ml	=	1 cup
300 ml	=	1¼ cups
375 ml	=	1½ cups
500 ml	=	2 cups
750 ml	=	3 cups
1 litre	=	4 cups

flavouring suggestions

beef: horseradish, ginger, black pepper, French mustard

lamb: mint, rosemary, chilli powder, garlic, turmeric, lemon juice

pork: orange juice, ginger, garlic, spring onions

fish: black pepper, lemon juice, parsley, dill

chicken: lemon juice, garlic, paprika, coriander, cumin

rice: saffron, garlic, onion

potatoes: chives, spring onions, dill, parsley, turmeric

carrots: orange juice, coriander, chives

tomatoes: basil, origanum, marjoram

green beans: lemon juice, mustard seeds

vitamins

vitamin A
artichokes, broccoli, carrots, Chinese cabbage, kale, red peppers, spinach, spring onions, sweet potatoes, watercress

vitamin B1
almonds, asparagus, brown rice, garlic, kelp, lentils, potatoes, soya beans and their products, wheat germ

vitamin B2
beetroot, lentils, millet, mushrooms, rye, sesame seeds, soya beans and their products, sunflower seeds, wheat

vitamin B12
cheese, eggs, meat, milk, oysters, liver, sea vegetables

vitamin C
asparagus, beetroot, carrot tops, fruit, green peppers, green leafy vegetables (broccoli), kale, watercress

vitamin D
dried fish, fresh vegetables, sunlight (this is the best source of this vitamin)

vitamin E
beans, brown rice and all whole grain cereals, carrots, celery, leeks, nuts, parsley, sweet potatoes

vitamin F
vegetable oils (including sesame and olive oil)

vitamin K
brown rice, cabbage, parsley, this vitamin is also produced by the intestinal flora

minerals

calcium
broccoli, cheese, Chinese cabbage, milk, parsley, sardines, sesame seeds, sea vegetables, spinach, sunflower/poppy seeds, tofu, yoghurt

magnesium
beetroot, cabbage, lentils, sea vegetables, spinach, soya beans and their products, watercress

phosphorus
artichokes, beans, broccoli, garlic, mushrooms, nuts, sea vegetables, wholegrain cereals

potassium
artichokes, bamboo shoots, beetroot, broccoli, butternut, cabbage, cauliflower, celery, dried fruits, garlic, nuts, parsley, parsnips, potatoes, pumpkin, sea vegetables, soya beans and their products, spinach

iron
beans, brown rice, kale, leeks, spinach, parsley, sea vegetables, sesame seeds, spring onions

iodine
green leafy vegetables, sea vegetables

sodium
beetroot, celery, dried fruits, corn on the cob, pickled cucumber, radish leaves, sea salt, sea vegetables

guide to fresh produce

spring
Vegetables: cabbages, leeks, asparagus, radishes, turnips, broccoli, peas, parsley
Fruits: apples, pears

summer
Vegetables: aubergines, beetroot, cabbages, carrots, cauliflower, celery, courgettes, onions, asparagus, radishes, spinach, turnips, cucumber, green beans, lettuce, marrow, corn on the cob, tomatoes, potatoes, runner beans, peas, parsley, garlic, squash
Fruits: apples, pears, plums, cherries, strawberries, blackberries, raspberries, gooseberries, blackcurrants

autumn
Vegetables: aubergines, beetroot, carrots, cauliflower, celery, courgettes, leeks, onions, radishes, spinach, turnips, cucumber, green beans, lettuce, marrow, tomatoes, potatoes, brussel sprouts, parsnips, peas, squash
Fruits: apples, pears, plums, cherries, strawberries, blackberries, raspberries

winter
Vegetables: cabbages, cauliflower, celery, leeks, turnips, broccoli, brussel sprouts, parsnips
Fruits: Apples, pears

preparation tips

how to julienne vegetables
Start by cutting a thin slice off one side of the vegetable so that you can lie it flat on the cutting surface. Place the vegetable flat-side down and cut the food lengthwise into slices, then cut each slice into narrow strips.

how to prepare avocado
Cut the avocado lengthwise around the pip. Gently twist the halves in opposite directions to separate them.

To remove the pip, carefully tap it with the blade of a sharp knife, so that the blade is caught in the pip. Rotate the knife to lift out the pip.

To peel the avocado, hold it – cut side down – in your hand and peel away the skin.

how to make a flower or tulip garnish using soft fruits
Choose a large tomato or fig (or similar fruit) and insert a sharp knife point at the top of the fruit, up to the centre. Cut six wedges from the top (as you would cut a pie), slicing downwards but not all the way through the bottom. These wedges, when separated at the top, will enable you to open the tomato outwards creating petals.

Use small vegetables or fruit as a garnish on top of a fresh salad or around the sides of a fruit, vegetable or meat platter. Larger vegetables or fruit can be stuffed with cottage cheese.

how to make vegetable and fruit fans
Peel the fruit or vegetable, remove any seeds or pips and cut it in half. Place one half – cut side down – on a cutting board, place a knife 1 cm away from top and cut lengthwise. Place on a plate and press down gently to spread the slices and create a fan shape.
Types of vegetables or fruits to use: apricots, avocados, gherkins, mangoes, papayas (papaws), peaches, radishes

quick reference to cooking methods

steam-frying

Use a heavy-based, non-stick pan or pot with a lid over medium heat.

Add a little non-stick spray if desired to prevent sticking. A little stock, water or wine can also be added to ingredients.

Gently fry ingredients, stirring occasionally, and replacing the lid each time to allow further cooking.

Foods suitable for steam-frying: meat or chicken, seafood, vegetables, fruits and eggs.

stir-frying

Use a heavy-based, non-stick frying pan or wok over medium heat. Add a little stock or water to ingredients while stirring to prevent sticking. Gently fry ingredients until crisp or lightly browned, according to the recipe.

Foods suitable for stir-frying: thinly sliced meat or chicken, seafood, vegetables, fruits, cooked pasta or rice.

dry-frying

Use a heavy-based, non-stick frying pan over medium heat. Add a little non-stick spray if desired to prevent sticking. A little stock, water or wine can also be added to ingredients while stirring to prevent sticking.

Gently fry ingredients, stirring, until crisp or lightly browned, according to the recipe.

Foods suitable for dry-frying: meat or chicken, seafood, vegetables, fruits and eggs.

baking

Preheat the oven according to the recipe, or to the average setting of 180 °C (350 °F).

Use a casserole dish. Add a little stock, water, wine or marinade to ingredients, or follow the recipe.

Cover with a casserole lid or aluminium foil, or cook uncovered, according to the recipe.

Foods suitable for baking: meat or chicken, seafood, vegetables, fruits and pasta.

roasting

Preheat the oven according to the recipe, or to the average setting of 180 °C (350 °F).

Use a casserole dish or roasting pan. Add a little stock, water, wine or marinade to ingredients, or follow the recipe.

Cover with a casserole lid or aluminium foil, or cook uncovered as per the recipe. Alternatively, use a roasting bag.

Foods suitable for roasting: lamb, beef, pork, chicken and vegetables.

poaching

Food can either be lowered into simmering liquid or it can be placed in the pan and the liquid can be added and heated until simmering. The liquid should almost cover the food, not submerge it. The pan can be covered or uncovered.

Foods suitable for poaching: eggs, seafood, chicken and fruits.

grilling

Preheat the grill or oven on the highest setting. Place the food on the grill rack and grill according to the recipe. With experience it will become easier to determine when meat is rare, medium or well-done. Rare steak is quite spongy and soft to the touch.

Foods suitable for grilling: lamb, beef, pork, chicken, seafood, vegetables and fruits.

juices & smoothies

Drink all fresh juices immediately as nutritional value is lost when refrigerated.

papaya smoothie

1½ apples, peeled, cored and chopped
juice of ½ lime or lemon
1 cm piece root ginger
½ papaya (papaw), peeled and seeds removed

Blend the apples, lime and ginger together.
Chop the papaya and add to the blender.
Add a little chilled still mineral water to the juice
if the consistency is too thick. **Makes 1 glass**

pineapple and pear smoothie

1 pear, peeled and chopped
1 apple, peeled, cored and chopped
1 thick slice pineapple, chopped

Blend all the ingredients together. Add a little chilled still mineral water to the juice if the consistency is too thick. **Makes 1 glass**

banana and pear shake

2 small pears, peeled and chopped
1 banana, sliced
90 ml (6 tablespoons) skim (fat-free) milk

Blend the pears, then add and blend the banana and milk. **Makes 1 glass**

carrot smoothie

2 large carrots, peeled and sliced
1 avocado, peeled and chopped
1 sprig fresh coriander, chopped

Blend the carrots, then add and blend the avocado and coriander. Add a little chilled still mineral water to the juice if the consistency is too thick. **Makes 1 glass**

carrot and celery smoothie

1 tomato, skinned and chopped
2 sticks celery, sliced
2–3 large carrots, peeled and sliced
juice of ½ lemon
1 sprig fresh parsley

Blend the tomato, celery, carrots and lemon juice. Pour into a glass and top with a sprig of parsley. Add a little chilled still mineral water to the juice if the consistency is too thick. **Makes 1 glass**

grape ripple

1½ apples, peeled, cored and chopped
20 white grapes
10 red grapes

Blend the apples and grapes and pour into a glass. Add a little chilled still mineral water to the juice if the consistency is too thick. **Makes 1 glass**

breakfast drinks

mango and pineapple shake

1 mango, peeled and sliced
2 slices pineapple, chopped
1 banana, sliced
125 ml (½ cup) skim (fat-free) milk

Blend all the ingredients together. **Makes 1 glass**

tomato and celery smoothie

3 tomatoes, skinned and chopped
2 sticks celery, sliced
1 sprig fresh coriander

Blend all the ingredients together. Add a little chilled still mineral water to the juice if the consistency is too thick. **Makes 1 glass**

grapefruit splash

1 grapefruit, peeled and chopped
1 orange, peeled and chopped
6 cherries, pits removed
125 ml (½ cup) still mineral water

Blend all the ingredients together. **Makes 1 glass**

mango and carrot juice

1 carrot, peeled and sliced
1 mango, peeled and sliced
125 ml (½ cup) still mineral water

Blend all the ingredients together. **Makes 1 glass**

pineapple and banana shake

1 banana, sliced
2 slices pineapple, chopped
125 ml (½ cup) skim (fat-free) milk

Blend all the ingredients together. **Makes 1 glass**

peach blend

2 peaches, peeled and pips removed
5 ml (1 teaspoon) clear honey
30 ml (2 tablespoons) fat-free
or low-fat plain yoghurt
60 ml (¼ cup) skim (fat-free) milk

Chop the peaches and blend. Add the honey, yoghurt and milk to the peach mixture and blend. Makes 1 glass

lunchtime drinks

strawberry blend

1 pear, peeled and chopped
1 handful strawberries, cleaned and hulled
125 ml (½ cup) still mineral water

Blend all the ingredients together. **Makes 1 glass**

apricot smoothie

3 apricots, chopped
60 ml (¼ cup) fat-free or low-fat plain yoghurt
105 ml (7 tablespoons) skim (fat-free) milk

Blend all the ingredients together. **Makes 1 glass**

FROM FRONT TO BACK: *Beetroot Blend (p. 17),
Pineapple and Banana Shake (this page)
and Strawberry Blend (this page).*

cucumber mix

¼ large English cucumber, peeled and sliced
4 broccoli florets
2 tomatoes, skinned and chopped

Blend all the ingredients together. Add a little chilled still mineral water to the juice if the consistency is too thick. **Makes 1 glass**

papaya and pear smoothie

½ papaya (papaw), peeled and seeds removed
2 small pears, peeled and chopped

Chop the papaya and blend. Add the pears to the mixture and blend. Add a little chilled still mineral water to the juice if the consistency is too thick. **Makes 1 glass**

carrot and apple juice

1 apple, peeled, cored and chopped
1 carrot, peeled and sliced
125 ml (½ cup) still mineral water

Blend all the ingredients together. **Makes 1 glass**

watermelon juice

¼ watermelon, peeled and seeds removed
125 ml (½ cup) still mineral water

Chop the watermelon and blend with the water. **Makes 1 glass**

dinner drinks

mango shake

1 mango, peeled and sliced
1 nectarine, peeled and sliced
125 ml (½ cup) skim (fat-free) milk

Blend all the ingredients together. **Makes 1 glass**

melon mix

1 small melon, peeled and seeds removed
pinch of ground cinnamon

Chop the melon, sprinkle with cinnamon and blend. Add a little chilled still mineral water to the juice if the consistency is too thick. **Makes 1 glass**

grapefruit mix

1½ grapefruits, peeled and chopped
1 lime or lemon, peeled,
pips removed and chopped

Blend the ingredients together. Add a little chilled still mineral water to the juice if the consistency is too thick. **Makes 1 glass**

beetroot blend

¼ medium beetroot, peeled and chopped
2 large carrots, peeled and sliced
2 sprigs fresh basil

Blend all the ingredients together. Add a little chilled still mineral water to the juice if the consistency is too thick. **Makes 1 glass**

tomato blend

3 tomatoes, skinned and chopped
¼ large English cucumber, peeled and sliced
6 spinach leaves

Blend all the ingredients together. Add a little chilled still mineral water to the juice if the consistency is too thick. **Makes 1 glass**

peppers and carrot blend

½ green pepper, seeded and chopped
½ red pepper, seeded and chopped
2 large carrots, peeled and sliced

Blend all the ingredients together. Add a little chilled still mineral water to the juice if the consistency is too thick. **Makes 1 glass**

breakfasts

baked french toast

180 ml (¾ cup) fat-free or low-fat smooth
or chunky plain cottage cheese
60 ml (¼ cup) skim (fat-free) milk
30 ml (2 tablespoons) brown sugar
1 large egg
1 large egg white
3 ml (½ teaspoon) vanilla essence
4 thin slices whole-wheat or whole grain bread

Preheat the oven to 220 ˚C (425 ˚F).
Blend the cottage cheese, milk, sugar, egg, egg white and
vanilla essence for about 1 minute or until smooth.
Transfer the mixture to a shallow dish, place the bread
in it and leave to stand for 10 minutes. Turn the bread over
and leave it to stand for another 10 minutes.
Meanwhile, grease a baking sheet with non-stick spray
and place in the oven for 7 minutes.
Remove the baking sheet, place bread on it and bake for 6 minutes.
Turn the bread and bake for another 5–6 minutes,
or until golden brown.
Serve with sugar-free jam or a savoury topping. **Serves 4**

scrambled egg and mushrooms

125 ml (½ cup) button mushrooms, halved
15 ml (1 tablespoon) olive oil or non-stick spray
30 ml (2 tablespoons) light soy sauce
freshly ground black pepper to taste
2 eggs*, beaten
1 small bunch mustard cress, finely chopped

Heat the oil in a non-stick pan and fry mushrooms, or dry-fry using non-stick spray, for 2 minutes, stirring.

Add the soy sauce and season with black pepper. Stir and cook for another minute.

Transfer the mushrooms to a plate, wipe out the pan with kitchen paper and return to the heat until hot. Coat with non-stick spray.

Season the eggs with pepper only, and stir into the hot pan. Scramble until set, then mix in the mushrooms. Serve topped with mustard cress. **Serves 2**

* You can also use one whole egg and one egg white, or just 2 egg whites.

tomatoes on pesto toast

5 ml (1 teaspoon) margarine or fat-free plain cottage cheese
10 ml (2 teaspoons) pesto sauce
1 large, ripe tomato
1 slice whole-wheat or granary bread
salt and freshly ground black pepper to taste

Preheat the grill. Mix together the margarine or cottage cheese and pesto sauce.

Halve the tomato widthwise and season well. Grill for 3 minutes.

Lightly toast the bread, then spread half the pesto mix on the toast. Top with the tomato halves. Divide the remaining pesto between the tomato halves, sprinkle with seasoning and serve. **Serves 1**

orange, grapefruit and kiwi salad

1 large orange, peeled and pith removed, quartered
1 pink grapefruit, peeled and pith removed, quartered
1 kiwi fruit, peeled and sliced
small handful seedless grapes
pinch of dried mint

Divide the fruit between two bowls, and sprinkle with mint. Chill for 1 hour before serving. **Serves 2**

dried fruit compote

1 x 250 g packet dried fruit mix
375 ml (1½ cups) water
1 whole dried clove
pinch of mixed spice
pinch of ground cinnamon

Cover the fruit with water. Add the spices and bring the mixture to the boil. Reduce heat and simmer for about 20 minutes, or until fruit is plump and most of the liquid reduced. **Serves 4**

Note: As an alternative, use orange juice or apple juice instead of water.

yoghurt and fruit

15 ml (1 tablespoon) porridge oats
180 ml (¾ cup) fat-free or low-fat plain yoghurt
10 ml (2 teaspoons) clear honey
1 banana, sliced
3 strawberries, sliced
pinch of ground cinnamon

Heat a small non-stick frying pan until hot, and dry-fry oats for 2 minutes, stirring. Set aside oats to cool.

Mix the yoghurt and honey and spoon into a glass. Top with banana and strawberry slices and sprinkle with cinnamon and toasted oats before serving. **Serves 1**

boiled egg with relish

1 large free-range egg
30–60 ml (2–4 tablespoons) tomato
and onion relish
1 slice whole-wheat or
wholegrain bread, toasted
salt and freshly ground black pepper to taste
5 ml (1 tablespoon) chopped fresh parsley

Place the egg in a saucepan of boiling water.

For soft boiled egg boil for 3–4 minutes; for hard boiled egg boil for 5–6 minutes.

Peel the shell off the egg when cooked.

Towards the end of the egg cooking time, toast the bread, then spread with the tomato and onion relish. Slice the boiled egg and layer it on top of the relish. Season to taste and garnish with a sprinkling of parsley. **Serves 1**

Note: If the shell cracks while boiling, add a little salt to the water. It firms the white and prevents the egg from escaping through the shell.

If poaching eggs, add a few drops of vinegar to the water and they will set more quickly.

soups

chinese chicken and mushroom soup

1 litre (4 cups) water
180 ml (¾ cup) canned bamboo shoots, drained
4 large dried shiitake mushrooms (optional)
250 g chicken breasts, skinned, deboned and cut into strips
500 ml (2 cups) button mushrooms, sliced
3 spring onions, chopped
1 chicken stock cube
45 ml (3 tablespoons) soy sauce
10 ml (2 teaspoons) honey
±20 ml (4 heaped teaspoons) cornflour
250 g tofu (soya bean curd), cut into strips
30 ml (2 tablespoons) rice vinegar or white wine vinegar
2 ml (¼ teaspoon) Tabasco sauce

Bring 250 ml (1 cup) of water to the boil. Place bamboo shoots in
a bowl, pour half the boiling water over them, and soak for
5 minutes. Drain. If using the shiitake mushrooms, soak for
15 minutes in the remaining boiled water. Drain and reserve liquid.
Slice the mushrooms and discard the stems.
Place a little water and the chicken in a saucepan and stir for
4 minutes. Add the bamboo shoots, shiitake mushrooms, button
mushrooms, spring onions, stock cube, soy sauce, honey and
reserved liquid. Bring to the boil, reduce heat and simmer.
In a small bowl, mix the cornflour with the remaining water
and stir the mixture into the soup. Cook for 5 minutes.
Stir in the tofu, vinegar and Tabasco, and cook until
the tofu is heated through. Serve immediately. **Serves 4–6**

Note: Shiitake mushrooms have medicinal properties. They are dried
and imported from Japan. Tofu is a soya bean curd made from soya
beans and nigari, a coagulant taken from crude salt. It is high in
protein, and can be used in soups, vegetable dishes and dressings.

vegetable stock

1 litre (4 cups) water
500 ml (2 cups) chopped fresh vegetables
of your choice

Bring the water to the boil, add the vegetables and simmer until the vegetables are cooked. Remove the vegetables and reserve the water (stock).

Boil stock rapidly in an uncovered saucepan until it is reduced to a little less than half the original quantity. Strain and cool. The stock can be frozen for future use, or it can be refrigerated in a covered container for up to five days.

Use the stock as a base for soups or instead of water and stock cubes in recipes.

Variations:
Celery, fennel and onions
Garlic, parsley and leeks

croûtons

4 slices whole-wheat or whole grain bread

Preheat the oven to 180 °C (350 °F).

Cut the bread into bite-sized cubes. Bake for about 15 minutes, or until golden brown and crunchy. **Serves 2–4**

Note: Croûtons can be added to soup or to green salad just before serving.

vegetable soup

1 onion, chopped
3 sticks celery, sliced
3 large potatoes, peeled and cubed
10 ml (2 teaspoons) Marmite dissolved in 1 litre
(4 cups) boiling water
salt and freshly ground black pepper to taste
500 ml (2 cups) chopped fresh vegetables

Place onion, celery, potatoes, Marmite water and seasoning in a saucepan. Bring to the boil, then simmer until the potatoes are tender.

Add seasonal vegetables and simmer for a further 10 minutes, or until soft. Season.

To thicken the soup, remove the potatoes and blend, then stir back into the soup. **Serves 4**

cold tomato-buttermilk soup

750 ml (3 cups) canned tomato soup
250 ml (1 cup) buttermilk
10 ml (2 teaspoons) grated orange rind
125 ml (½ cup) freshly squeezed orange juice
2 ml (¼ teaspoon) ground allspice
2 ml (¼ teaspoon) ground nutmeg

In a large bowl, mix all the ingredients together until well blended. Cover and refrigerate until cold (about 2 hours). Serve chilled. Garnish with mint if desired. **Serves 4**

clear vegetable soup

4 carrots, cut into long strips (julienned)
2–4 turnips, peeled and cut into long strips (julienned)
2–4 leeks, cut into long strips (julienned)
1 litre (4 cups) salted water
45 ml (3 tablespoons) Marmite
or 1 vegetable stock cube
salt and freshly ground black pepper to taste

Cover the vegetables with salted water and bring to the boil. When cooked but still crisp remove the vegetables and place in cold water to preserve their colour.

In the meantime, dissolve the Marmite or stock cube in the remaining boiling water, and return the vegetables to this stock. Serve immediately. **Serves 3**

lemon soup

1.5 litres (6 cups) vegetable stock (see page 24)
250 ml (1 cup) cooked long-grain brown rice
juice of 1 lemon
250 ml (1 cup) cubed tofu (soya bean curd)
5 ml (1 teaspoon) grated lemon rind
salt and freshly ground black pepper to taste

Bring the stock to the boil, then stir in the cooked rice. Add the lemon juice and tofu, and simmer for 10 minutes. Add the grated lemon rind and simmer for a further 2 minutes. Season. Serve hot. **Serves 4**

butternut soup

2 x 500 g butternuts, peeled and cubed
1.25 litres (5 cups) water
5 ml (1 teaspoon) vegetable stock powder
5 ml (1 teaspoon) ground cinnamon
30 ml (2 tablespoons) honey (optional)

Bring all the ingredients to the boil, then simmer until the butternut is tender. Blend the soup for a creamier texture or serve immediately. **Serves 4–6**

Note: Curry powder (to taste) can be added to the butternut soup for a spicy alternative.

chicken and vegetable soup

1 onion, chopped
1 clove garlic, chopped
2 chicken breast fillets, cubed
500 g chopped fresh vegetables (potatoes, celery, leeks, carrots, broccoli, cabbage, turnips)
250 ml (1 cup) canned tomatoes
2 ml (¼ teaspoon) Tabasco sauce (optional)
1 vegetable stock cube
salt and freshly ground black pepper to taste

Steam-fry the onion and garlic with the chicken. Add the chopped vegetables, tomatoes and just enough water to cover. Add Tabasco if desired. Add the stock cube and seasoning to the mixture, cover and simmer gently on low until the vegetables are cooked. **Serves 4–6**

thick vegetable soup

1 leek, chopped
1 onion, chopped
1 clove garlic, chopped
1 stick celery, sliced
4 carrots, peeled and sliced
1 parsnip, chopped
2 turnips, peeled and chopped
1.5 litres (6 cups) water
1 vegetable stock cube
2 bay leaves
180 ml (¾ cup) brown rice
500 ml (2 cups) peas
250 ml (1 cup) green beans, chopped
salt and freshly ground black pepper to taste
2 ml (¼ teaspoon) Tabasco sauce (optional)
30 ml (2 tablespoons) chopped fresh parsley

Steam-fry the leek, onion and garlic. Add the celery, carrots, parsnip and turnips. Cover and leave to sweat for 5 minutes. Add the water, vegetable stock, bay leaves and rice, and cook for 30 minutes. Add the peas and beans, and cook for a further 15 minutes.

Season and add Tabasco sauce if desired. Sprinkle with parsley and serve immediately. Serves 4–6

Butternut Soup

salads & dressings

salads

tomato and orange salad

1 large orange, peeled and pith removed
4 tomatoes, cut into wedges
½ small red or white onion, thinly sliced
60 g fresh baby leaf spinach
or cos lettuce, shredded
15 ml (1 tablespoon) fat-free French dressing
salt and freshly ground black pepper to taste

Cut the orange into the same size chunks as the tomatoes.
Mix with the onion, spinach and dressing.
Season well and chill slightly before serving. **Serves 4**

grated carrot salad

3 carrots, peeled and coarsely grated
30 ml (2 tablespoons) sultanas (optional)
juice of 1 small lemon
30 ml (2 tablespoons) chopped fresh mint
or parsley
salt and freshly ground black pepper to taste

Mix together the carrots, sultanas (if using), lemon juice and herbs. Season well and chill slightly before serving. **Serves 1–2**

grated cucumber salad

1 English cucumber
salt and freshly ground black pepper to taste
2 small onions, finely chopped
45 ml (3 tablespoons) fat-free
or low-fat plain yoghurt
5 ml (1 teaspoon) dried dill

Halve the cucumber lengthwise, scoop out the seeds with a teaspoon and coarsely grate the flesh. Season lightly and mix with the onions, yoghurt and dill. **Serves 2**

grated beetroot salad

2 whole cooked beetroots, cooled
1 large apple, peeled
10 ml (2 teaspoons) olive oil
15 ml (1 tablespoon) red or white wine vinegar
salt and freshly ground black pepper to taste

Drain the beetroots and pat dry with kitchen paper. Core and quarter the apple. Coarsely grate the beetroot and the apple, then mix in the oil, vinegar and seasoning. Chill before serving. **Serves 2**

orange and carrot salad

1 serving small green salad
1 large orange, peeled and pith removed
30 ml (2 tablespoons) fat-free
or low-fat smooth plain cottage cheese
30 ml (2 tablespoons) peeled and grated carrot

Arrange the green salad on a plate. Slice the orange into rounds and arrange on top of the green salad. Spoon the cottage cheese into the centre and pile the grated carrot on top. Serve with Orange and Lemon Vinaigrette (see page 38). **Serves 1**

apple and tuna salad

125 ml (½ cup) tuna in brine, drained
1 large Starking apple, cored and chopped
(do not peel)
2 sticks celery, sliced
1 small lettuce, shredded
1 handful bean sprouts
15 ml (1 tablespoon) fat-free
or low-fat mayonnaise
125 ml (½ cup) fat-free or low-fat plain yoghurt

Combine the tuna with the apple, celery, lettuce and bean sprouts. Add the mayonnaise and yoghurt and mix into the salad. **Serves 2–4**

mushroom, courgette and tomato salad

6 large brown mushrooms, sliced
4 courgettes (baby marrows), thinly sliced
4 tomatoes, quartered
5 ml (1 teaspoon) chopped fresh basil
salt and freshly ground black pepper to taste
1 bunch watercress, trimmed and
divided into sprigs

Combine the mushrooms, courgettes and tomatoes in a salad bowl and sprinkle with basil. Season. Arrange the sprigs of watercress around the edge of the salad. **Serves 4**

Note: The mushrooms and courgettes can be grilled first if desired.

mixed vegetable salad

1 large lettuce, shredded
1 floret each broccoli and cauliflower, broken
into bite-sized pieces
4–6 carrots, peeled and sliced
1 avocado, peeled, cubed and
soaked in lemon juice
1 stick celery, sliced
1 small onion, sliced or 125 ml (½ cup) chopped
spring onions
250 ml (1 cup) button mushrooms, halved
salt and freshly ground black pepper to taste

Combine all the salad ingredients and refrigerate until ready to serve. **Serves 4–6**

crunchy salad

4 lettuce leaves, shredded
1 large tomato, sliced
1 English cucumber, chopped
2 sticks celery, sliced
1 green or red pepper, seeded and diced
125 ml (½ cup) peas
2 spring onions, chopped
snipped chives to garnish
60 ml (¼ cup) lemon juice
salt and freshly ground black pepper to taste

Divide the lettuce between two plates. Arrange the tomato, cucumber, celery, pepper, peas and spring onions on top of the lettuce. Sprinkle over chives to garnish. Pour over lemon juice and season just before serving. **Serves 2**

coleslaw

225 g white cabbage, trimmed and grated
4–6 carrots, peeled and grated
½ onion, grated
180 ml (¾ cup) fat-free dressing
salt and freshly ground black pepper to taste

Combine all the ingredients and chill well before serving. **Serves 4**

Vegetable Salad

bean and yoghurt salad

1 x 410 g can butter beans, drained
375 ml (1½ cups) button mushrooms, sliced
4 spring onions, chopped
180 ml (¾ cup) fat-free or low-fat plain yoghurt
salt and freshly ground black pepper to taste

Combine the beans, mushrooms and onions with the yoghurt. Season well and chill. **Serves 4**

bean and vegetable salad

60 ml (¼ cup) canned butter beans, drained
60 ml (¼ cup) bean sprouts
60 ml (¼ cup) sliced courgettes (baby marrows)
60 ml (¼ cup) chopped apple
60 ml (¼ cup) seedless raisins
salt and freshly ground black pepper to taste

Combine the beans, bean sprouts, courgettes, apple and raisins. Season and serve with a fat-free French dressing. **Serves 2**

brown rice and vegetable salad

750 ml (3 cups) cooked brown rice
2 spring onions, chopped
2 sticks celery, finely sliced
1 carrot, peeled and finely sliced
2 tomatoes, chopped
½ green pepper, seeded and finely chopped
½ red pepper, seeded and finely chopped
salt and freshly ground black pepper to taste

Mix all the salad ingredients in a large bowl and season well. Serve with a vinaigrette dressing. **Serves 4**

apple, honey and ginger salad

6 Granny Smith apples, cored and cubed
(do not peel)
60 ml (¼ cup) freshly squeezed orange juice
5 ml (1 teaspoon) grated fresh ginger
10 ml (2 teaspoons) clear honey
2 tomatoes, chopped
45 ml (3 tablespoons) toasted sesame seeds
(optional)

Place the cubed apples in a salad bowl.

Mix together the orange juice, ginger and honey, and pour over the apples immediately to prevent them from turning brown. Add the tomatoes to the apple salad and mix in the sesame seeds if desired. **Serves 4**

bean sprout salad

250 ml (1 cup) bean sprouts
2 carrots, peeled and cut into strips (julienned)
1 stick celery, finely sliced
1 red pepper, seeded and finely chopped
2 spring onions, finely chopped
salt and freshly ground black pepper to taste

Mix all the salad ingredients in a large bowl and season well. Serve with a vinaigrette or avocado dressing (see page 39). **Serves 2**

brown rice salad

500 ml (2 cups) cooked brown rice
2 spring onions, finely chopped
1 clove garlic, crushed
125 ml (½ cup) grated pineapple
125 ml (½ cup) cored and
chopped Granny Smith apple
125 ml (½ cup) tangerine or orange segments
125 ml (½ cup) seedless raisins (optional)
1 lettuce, shredded
salt and freshly ground black pepper to taste

Mix all the salad ingredients in a large bowl and season well. Served with lemon juice or a vinaigrette dressing. **Serves 2–4**

pasta, apple and pepper salad

250 ml (1 cup) pasta, cooked and drained
125 ml (½ cup) cored and
chopped Granny Smith apple
½ red pepper, seeded and finely chopped
½ green pepper, seeded and finely chopped
1 spring onion, finely chopped
salt and freshly ground black pepper to taste

Mix all the salad ingredients in a large bowl and season well. Serve with a dressing of your choice. Serves 2

dressings

As an alternative to salad dressing, try drizzling one of the following over a salad of your choice: balsamic vinegar, wine vinegar, lemon juice, orange juice, pineapple juice or plain fat-free yoghurt.

cottage cheese dressing

250 ml (1 cup) fat-free plain yoghurt
or buttermilk
60 ml (¼ cup) fat-free smooth plain
cottage cheese
3 ml (½ teaspoon) mustard powder
15 ml (1 tablespoon) lemon juice
5 ml (1 teaspoon) honey
5 ml (1 teaspoon) finely chopped fresh parsley
45 ml (3 tablespoons) finely snipped fresh chives
1 clove garlic, crushed
salt and freshly ground black pepper to taste

Combine all the ingredients in a blender and chill before serving. **Makes 300 ml (1¼ cups)**

creamy tomato vinaigrette

1 large tomato, skinned, quartered and seeded
125 ml (½ cup) tomato juice
125 ml (½ cup) fat-free or low-fat plain yoghurt
30 ml (2 tablespoons) fat-free or low-fat
mayonnaise or oil-free creamy salad dressing
a few drops Tabasco sauce

Blend the tomato and tomato juice for 30 seconds, or until smooth. Add the yoghurt, mayonnaise or salad dressing and Tabasco, and blend for about 30 seconds, or until well combined. This dressing can be kept for up to three days if refrigerated. **Makes 375 ml (1½ cups)**

honey and mustard dressing

125 ml (½ cup) balsamic vinegar
25 ml (5 teaspoons) French mustard
15 ml (1 tablespoon) clear, thin honey
salt and freshly ground black pepper to taste

Place all the ingredients in a sealed container and shake well. This dressing has a rather strong flavour so use it in small quantities. **Makes 180 ml (¾ cup)**

Cottage Cheese Dressing

tangy yoghurt dressing

180 ml (¾ cup) fat-free or low-fat plain yoghurt
5 ml (1 teaspoon) finely grated lemon rind
5 ml (1 teaspoon) lemon juice
5 ml (1 teaspoon) French mustard
5 ml (1 teaspoon) clear honey
salt and freshly ground black pepper to taste

Place all the ingredients into a sealed container and shake well. **Makes 180 ml (¾ cup)**

oil-free dressing

250 ml (1 cup) apple juice
125 ml (½ cup) apple cider vinegar
2 cloves garlic, crushed
5 ml (1 teaspoon) dried mixed herbs
pinch each of dried thyme and dried origanum
salt and freshly ground black pepper to taste

Combine all the ingredients in a blender. Chill well before using. **Makes 375 ml (1½ cups)**

orange and lemon vinaigrette

125 ml (½ cup) wine vinegar
60 ml (¼ cup) lemon juice
60 ml (¼ cup) orange juice
3 ml (½ teaspoon) French mustard
pinch of crushed garlic
grated rind of 1 lemon
salt and freshly ground black pepper to taste

Place all the ingredients into a sealed container and shake well. Refrigerate. This dressing keeps for two days. **Makes 250 ml (1 cup)**

easy salad dressing

105 ml (7 tablespoons) cider vinegar
25 ml (5 teaspoons) lemon juice
15 ml (1 tablespoon) tomato sauce
15 ml (1 tablespoon) Worcestershire sauce
10 ml (2 teaspoons) soy sauce
1 clove garlic, minced
pinch of paprika
2 ml (¼ teaspoon) mustard powder
salt and freshly ground black pepper to taste
artificial sweetener to taste (optional)

Place all the ingredients into a sealed container and shake well. Chill before using. **Makes 165 ml (⅔ cup)**

herb salad dressing

250 ml (1 cup) fat-free or low-fat plain yoghurt,
or buttermilk
3 ml (½ teaspoon) mustard powder
15 ml (1 tablespoon) lemon juice
5 ml (1 teaspoon) clear, thin honey
5 ml (1 teaspoon) finely chopped fresh parsley
5 ml (1 teaspoon) finely chopped fresh tarragon
1 spring onion, finely chopped
1 clove garlic, crushed
salt and freshly ground black pepper to taste

Combine all the ingredients in a blender. Chill before serving. **Makes 250 ml (1 cup)**

avocado dressing

125 ml (½ cup) fat-free or low-fat plain yoghurt
1 avocado, peeled and chopped
salt and freshly ground black pepper to taste

Blend all the ingredients together. Chill before using. **Makes 250 ml (1 cup)**

light meals

fresh vegetable ideas

pepper wedges

500 ml–1 litre (2–4 cups) fat-free smooth plain cottage cheese
30 ml (2 tablespoons) lemon juice
30–60 ml (2–4 tablespoons) chopped fresh parsley
5 ml (1 teaspoon) snipped fresh chives
5 ml (1 teaspoon) chopped fresh dill
5 ml (1 teaspoon) chopped fresh basil
salt and freshly ground black pepper to taste
1 red pepper, seeded and quartered
1 green pepper, seeded and quartered
1 yellow pepper, seeded and quartered

Combine the cottage cheese, lemon juice, herbs and seasoning.
Fill the pepper quarters with the cheese mixture, arrange on
a platter and chill until ready to serve.
Serves 4–6

Note: If preferred, the peppers can be roasted first.
Other suitable vegetables are button mushroom caps,
celery sticks or chicory leaves.

cucumber spirals

1 English cucumber, cut into 1 cm thick slices
125 ml (½ cup) fat-free smooth plain
cottage cheese
125 ml (½ cup) feta cheese, cubed
6 slices ricotta cheese
freshly ground black pepper to taste
sprigs of fresh parsley to garnish

Top the cucumber rounds alternately with cottage cheese, feta and ricotta. Sprinkle with black pepper and garnish with parsley. **Serves 4–6**

Note: Add chopped spring onions and/or fresh herbs to the cottage cheese as an alternative.

chicory boats

4 chicory or endive leaves
125 ml (½ cup) fat-free smooth plain
cottage cheese
freshly ground black pepper to taste
chopped walnuts or pecan nuts to garnish
(optional)

Wash the chicory leaves. Spoon cottage cheese onto the leaves, sprinkle with pepper and top with chopped walnuts or pecan nuts if using. Arrange on a platter and serve with cherry tomatoes, celery or courgette (baby marrow) wedges. **Serves 4**

toast, baked potato & pasta toppings

basic white sauce

500 ml (2 cups) skim (fat-free) milk
salt and white pepper to taste
±20 ml (4 heaped teaspoons) cornflour

In a heavy-based saucepan, heat 450 ml milk with salt and pepper to near boiling point.

In a jug, mix the remaining milk and cornflour to a thin paste.

Remove the milk from heat before it starts to boil and add it to the cornflour paste while stirring quickly. Pour the sauce back into the saucepan, return to heat and bring to the boil, stirring all the time. Remove from heat when the sauce is thick and smooth. **Makes 500 ml (2 cups)**

chicken topping

150 g cooked chicken, chopped
30 ml (2 tablespoons) chopped fresh parsley
1 spring onion, finely chopped
salt and freshly ground black pepper to taste
500 ml (2 cups) white sauce (see page 42)

Combine the chicken, parsley and spring onion. Season well and stir into the white sauce. **Serves 4**

tuna topping

2 x 150 g cans tuna in water, drained
60 ml (¼ cup) tomato sauce
1 spring onion, finely chopped
1 green pepper, seeded and finely chopped
salt and freshly ground black pepper to taste
500 ml (2 cups) white sauce (see page 42)

Combine the tuna, tomato sauce, spring onion and green pepper. Season well and stir into the white sauce. **Serves 4**

mushroom sauce

500 ml (2 cups) button mushrooms,
left whole or sliced
1 small onion, finely chopped
1 clove garlic, crushed
salt and freshly ground black pepper to taste
500 ml (2 cups) white sauce (see page 42)

Dry-fry the mushrooms, onion and garlic in a heavy-based pan, using non-stick spray. Add seasoning. When heated through, stir the mixture into the white sauce. **Serves 4**

cottage cheese and sprouts

180 ml (¾ cup) fat-free or low-fat smooth plain
cottage cheese
handful alfalfa sprouts
handful chives, snipped
salt and freshly ground black pepper to taste

Mix all the ingredients together and spoon onto toasted whole-wheat or rye bread or use as a topping for baked potatoes. **Serves 2**

sandwich & baked potato fillings

hummus and sprouts

180 ml (¾ cup) hummus (chickpea spread)
handful alfalfa sprouts
60 ml (¼ cup) sliced English cucumber
salt and freshly ground black pepper to taste

Mix all ingredients together and spoon onto whole-wheat or rye bread or use as a topping for baked potatoes. **Serves 2**

chicken sandwich

30 ml (2 tablespoons) cottage cheese
and sprouts mixture (see page 43)
1–2 lettuce leaves
1 small, cooked chicken breast fillet,
skin removed and shredded
60 ml (¼ cup) sliced English cucumber
2–4 slices tomato
salt and freshly ground black pepper to taste
2 slices whole grain, whole-wheat or rye bread
or 1 whole-wheat pita

Spread the cottage cheese and sprouts mixture on both slices of bread. Layer the lettuce, chicken, cucumber and tomato onto one slice of the bread, and season to taste. Top with the remaining slice of bread and serve. **Serves 1**

tuna sandwich

30 ml (2 tablespoons) cottage cheese
and sprouts mixture (see page 43)
1–2 lettuce leaves
60 ml (¼ cup) tuna (or salmon) in brine, drained
60 ml (¼ cup) sliced English cucumber
salt and freshly ground black pepper to taste
2 slices whole grain, whole-wheat or rye bread
or 1 whole-wheat pita

Spread the cottage cheese and sprouts mixture on both slices of bread. Layer the lettuce, tuna and cucumber onto one slice of the bread, and season to taste. Top with the remaining slice of bread and serve. **Serves 1**

Chicken Sandwich

egg sandwich

30 ml (2 tablespoons) cottage cheese
and sprouts mixture (see page 43)
1–2 lettuce leaves
1 hard-boiled egg, sliced
60 ml (¼ cup) sliced English cucumber
2–4 slices tomato
salt and freshly ground black pepper to taste
2 slices whole grain, whole-wheat or rye bread,
or 1 whole-wheat pita

Spread the cottage cheese and sprouts mixture on both slices of bread. Layer the lettuce, egg, cucumber and tomato onto one slice of the bread, and season to taste. Top with the remaining slice of bread and serve. **Serves 1**

pancakes

basic pancake

250 ml (1 cup) cake flour
2 egg whites
300 ml (1¼ cups) water
15 ml (1 tablespoon) vinegar
pinch of salt

Mix all the ingredients together until smooth. Leave to stand for 30 minutes.

Grease a heavy-based, non-stick pan with non-stick spray and heat. Pour about 45 ml (3 tablespoons) pancake batter into the pan. Tilt pan to spread the mixture evenly. Lift the edges when golden, and turn the pancake to cook the other side. Serve with a filling of your choice. **Makes 6 pancakes**

easy cheese filling

2 x 250 g tubs fat-free smooth plain
cottage cheese
1 bunch garlic chives, snipped
5 ml (1 teaspoon) chopped fresh parsley
salt and freshly ground black pepper to taste

Mix all the ingredients together. Spoon generous amounts of the mixture into the pancakes.

Serve cold or place in a casserole and heat through. **Serves 6**

Other pancake filling ideas:
Fresh fruit, stewed fruit, baked fruit, sorbet, fruit purée or sauce, chicken, mince, fish, steam-fried vegetables, baked vegetables, savoury mashed potato, vegetable curry

dips

vegetable dip

125 ml (½ cup) fat-free or low-fat smooth plain
cottage cheese
30 ml (2 tablespoons) peeled,
seeded and chopped cucumber
15 ml (1 tablespoon) pickled relish
5 ml (1 teaspoon) snipped fresh chives
30 ml (2 tablespoons) grated carrot
salt to taste
skim (fat-free) milk

Combine the cottage cheese with cucumber, relish, chives and grated carrot. Add salt and a little milk to obtain dipping consistency. Serve with cherry tomatoes, celery or courgette (baby marrow) wedges. **Serves 2**

pineapple dip

125 ml (½ cup) fat-free or low-fat smooth plain
cottage cheese
30 ml (2 tablespoons) crushed pineapple,
drained
15 ml (1 tablespoon) buttermilk or sour cream
3 ml (½ teaspoon) salt
3 ml (½ teaspoon) toasted sesame seeds
(optional)

Combine all the ingredients and chill until needed. Serve with savoury biscuits or fresh vegetable slices. **Serves 2**

cucumber dip

90 ml (6 tablespoons) fat-free or low-fat
plain yoghurt
5 cm thick slice English cucumber,
peeled and seeded
salt to taste

Blend all ingredients together until smooth. Serve with cherry tomatoes, celery, courgette (baby marrow) wedges or any vegetable slices. **Serves 2**

fish

Cooking time depends on the thickness of the fish. Fillets that are 3 cm thick should cook for 3–4 minutes on each side. To check if the fish is cooked, gently pierce it with a fork. When the fish flakes easily it is ready to serve. If over-cooked it will be tough and dry, and will lose some of its flavour.

grilled fish with olive salsa

2 pieces sole or other firm white fish
10 ml (2 teaspoons) chopped fresh origanum
1 clove garlic, crushed
10 ml (2 teaspoons) soy sauce
125 ml (½ cup) lemon juice
salt and freshly ground black pepper to taste

olive salsa
2–4 large gherkins, chopped
30 ml (2 tablespoons) chopped capers
12 green olives, stoned and chopped
30 ml (2 tablespoons) pesto sauce
60 ml (¼ cup) chopped fresh parsley
2 cloves garlic, crushed
10 ml (2 teaspoons) lemon juice
4 ml (¾ teaspoon) sugar
salt and freshly ground black pepper to taste
fresh dill or basil (optional)

Preheat the oven to 180 °C (350 °F).
Grease a casserole dish with non-stick spray. Place the fish in the dish.
Mix the remaining ingredients together and spoon over the fish. Bake for about 5 minutes on each side. Mix all the salsa ingredients together. Fresh dill or basil (as much as you like) can also be added. Serve the salsa separately or spoon 15 ml (1 tablespoon) on top of each portion of fish. **Serves 2**

hake and potato bake

4 potatoes, peeled and cut into flat slices
1 kg frozen hake or other firm
white fish fillets
3 tomatoes, sliced
1 onion, finely chopped
10 ml (2 teaspoons) fish spice
10 ml (2 teaspoons) chopped fresh parsley
salt and freshly ground black pepper to taste
250 ml (1 cup) buttermilk
or fat-free plain yoghurt

Preheat the oven to 180 °C (350 °F) and grease a casserole dish with non-stick spray.

Boil potatoes until almost done, then drain.

Place the fish in the casserole dish, and arrange the tomato and onion on top. Add spice, parsley and seasoning. Arrange the potato slices on top, and season with salt and pepper.

Spoon half the buttermilk or yoghurt over the potato slices, and bake for 30 minutes.

Spoon the remaining buttermilk or yoghurt over the potato slices, and bake for a further 10–15 minutes, until golden brown. **Serves 6**

Note: Use 500 ml (2 cups) fat-free milk mixed with 1 x 62 g packet mushroom soup in place of the buttermilk/yoghurt.

chinese fish kebabs

1 kg firm white fish, filleted
juice of 1–2 oranges
juice of ½ lemon
60 ml (¼ cup) soy sauce
3 ml (½ teaspoon) finely chopped fresh ginger
or 5 ml (1 teaspoon) dried ginger
60 ml (¼ cup) toasted sesame seeds
15 ml (1 tablespoon) honey or sugar

Soak eight wooden skewers in water before use to prevent burning.

Cut the fish into 2 cm cubes or bite-sized chunks. Thread about 6 cubes of fish onto each skewer.

Mix the orange juice, lemon juice, soy sauce, ginger, sesame seeds and honey together. Pour the mixture over the fish and leave to marinate for 30 minutes.

Place the fish on a greased baking sheet and grill for 2 minutes. Turn the kebabs, baste with sauce, and grill for a further 2 minutes.

Heat the remaining sauce and spoon over kebabs. Serve with a salad or lightly steamed vegetables. **Serves 4**

Note: Cubed calamari steaks can be used as an alternative to the white fish.

Hake and Potato Bake

spicy fish grill

750 g hake, cod or other firm
white fish fillets
5 ml (1 teaspoon) ground cumin
5 ml (1 teaspoon) ground coriander
5 ml (1 teaspoon) ground cardamom
15 ml (1 tablespoon) lemon juice
250 ml (1 cup) fat-free or low-fat plain yoghurt
salt and freshly ground black pepper to taste

Preheat the oven to 180 °C (350 °F).

Grease a casserole dish with non-stick spray and place the fish in the dish.

Mix the remaining ingredients together and spoon over the fish.

Bake for about 5 minutes on each side, or until cooked. **Serves 4**

Note: Fish wrapped in foil steams in its own juices to tender flaky perfection, and is ideal for baking in the oven or on the barbecue.

thai baked fish

700 g hake, cod or other firm
white fish fillets
juice and grated rind of 1 lime
10–20 ml (2–4 teaspoons) grated fresh ginger
1–2 stalks lemon grass
2 cloves garlic, crushed
5 ml (1 teaspoon) soy sauce or tamari sauce
1–2 fresh chillies, seeded and finely chopped

Preheat the oven to 180 °C (350 °F).

Grease a casserole dish with non-stick spray and place the fillets in the dish.

Mix the remaining ingredients together and spoon over the fish. Cover with a lid and bake for about 5 minutes on each side, or until cooked. **Serves 4**

easy haddock

600 g skinned haddock loins or other
firm white fish
salt and freshly ground black pepper to taste
500 ml (2 cups) skim (fat-free) milk

Place the fish in a saucepan. Season well. Pour the milk over the fish.

Heat until near boiling point; reduce the heat and simmer for about 15 minutes, or until tender. Do not over-cook. **Serves 4**

steamed fish

2 hake, cod or other firm
white fish fillets
1 tomato, sliced
1 onion, sliced
5 ml (1 teaspoon) fish spice
30 ml (2 tablespoons) lemon juice
180 ml (¾ cup) fish or vegetable stock,
or 5 ml (1 teaspoon) fish or vegetable stock
powder dissolved in 180 ml (¾ cup) hot water

Preheat the oven to 180 °C (350 °F).

Grease a casserole dish with non-stick spray and place the fillets in the dish. Arrange the slices of tomato and onion on top of the fish. Add the spice, lemon juice and stock. Cover and steam for about 10–15 minutes, or until cooked. Serve with vegetables. **Serves 2**

tuna and rice bake

250 ml (1 cup) rice, uncooked
1 onion, finely chopped
1 green pepper, seeded and finely chopped
1 clove garlic, crushed
5 ml (1 teaspoon) Marmite dissolved in
60 ml (¼ cup) hot water
2 x 185 g cans tuna in brine, drained
500 ml (2 cups) water
1 x 62 g packet mushroom soup powder
salt and freshly ground black pepper to taste
15 ml (1 tablespoon) finely chopped
fresh parsley

Preheat the oven to 180 °C (350 °F). Grease a shallow ovenproof dish with non-stick spray.

Prepare the rice in the usual way until the grains are tender, then rinse under cold running water and drain well.

Fry the onion, green pepper and garlic using the Marmite and water solution, then add the tuna.

Meanwhile, bring the 500 ml (2 cups) water and mushroom soup powder to the boil, stirring frequently.

Add the tuna mixture and seasoning and mix.

Spoon half the rice into the dish, add a layer of tuna mixture, sprinkle with parsley, and repeat, ending with a layer of tuna mixture. Cover the dish and bake for 30 minutes. **Serves 6**

fish cakes

225 g hake, cod or other firm white
fish fillets, steamed
250 ml (1 cup) mashed potatoes
1 egg white
30 ml (2 tablespoons) finely chopped
fresh parsley
5 ml (1 teaspoon) prepared mustard

Mix together the fish and potatoes. Add the egg white and stir well, then add the parsley and mustard.

Wet your hands and form the mixture into fish cakes. Dry-fry in a non-stick pan until golden brown on each side. Serve with vegetables or Avocado Dressing (see page 39). **Serves 2**

tuna and pasta bake

1–2 onions, finely chopped
2 cloves garlic, crushed
5 ml (1 teaspoon) mushroom or vegetable stock
powder dissolved in 250 ml (1 cup) hot water
500 ml (2 cups) button mushrooms, halved
1 green pepper, seeded and finely chopped
1–2 fresh chillies, seeded and finely chopped
(optional)
500 ml (2 cups) basic white sauce (see page 42)
500 g macaroni, cooked and drained
30 ml (2 tablespoons) chopped fresh parsley
5 ml (1 teaspoon) dried mixed herbs
250 ml (1 cup) tuna in water, drained
salt and freshly ground black pepper to taste

Preheat the oven to 140 °C (275 °F).

Grease a casserole dish with non-stick spray and set aside.

In a heavy-based, non-stick pan, dry-fry the onions and garlic. Add the stock.

Add the mushrooms, green pepper and chilli, and simmer until the stock has reduced.

Add the white sauce, pasta, parsley, mixed herbs and tuna, and season to taste.

Pour the mixture into the casserole dish and bake for 10–15 minutes. **Serves 4–6**

Fish Cakes with Avocado Dressing (p. 39)

chicken

oriental chicken kebabs

marinade
15 ml (1 tablespoon) lemon juice
1 clove garlic, crushed
60 ml (¼ cup) fresh ginger, grated
30 ml (2 tablespoons) honey or artificial sweetener
250 ml (1 cup) soy sauce

kebabs
1 medium onion, quartered (cocktail onions can also be used)
1 green pepper, seeded and cut into bite-sized pieces
1 red pepper, seeded and cut into bite-sized pieces
250–500 ml (1–2 cups) button mushrooms, wiped but left whole
400 g chicken breasts, skinned, deboned and cubed
1 small can pineapple rings, cut into bite-sized pieces

Combine all the marinade ingredients and pour into a flat container.
Soak eight wooden skewers in water before use to prevent burning.
Thread onion, green and red peppers, mushrooms, chicken
and pineapple pieces alternately onto skewers, then place
the kebabs in marinade and refrigerate overnight.
Cook the kebabs under a moderate grill or on the barbecue,
turning from time to time to prevent burning.
Serve with rice or baked potatoes and salad. **Serves 4**

chicken stock

Reserve the stock in which chicken has been cooked, then boil it rapidly in an uncovered saucepan until it has reduced to slightly less than half the original quantity. Cool this more concentrated stock, and then freeze it for future use. This stock can be used as a base for soup, or instead of water and stock cubes or powder in any of these recipes.

chicken tandoori

4 chicken breasts (about 175 g each), skinned
1 clove garlic, crushed
15 ml (1 tablespoon) tandoori powder
375 ml (1½ cups) fat-free
or low-fat plain yoghurt
onion slices to garnish

Make incisions in the chicken breasts and rub with the garlic. Place the chicken in a large shallow bowl.

Mix the tandoori powder with the yoghurt and pour over the chicken. Cover and refrigerate for about 3 hours.

Preheat the grill.

Remove the chicken from the marinade and grill for 20 minutes, turning frequently and basting with the marinade until cooked through.

Transfer the chicken to a heated serving dish and garnish with onion slices. Serve on a bed of shredded lettuce with lemon or lime wedges. Serves 4–6

chicken à la king

30–60 ml (2–4 tablespoons) cornflour or cake flour
750 ml (3 cups) skim (fat-free) milk
60 ml (¼ cup) skim (fat-free) milk powder
5 ml (1 teaspoon) mushroom stock powder
5 ml (1 teaspoon) chicken stock powder
salt and freshly ground black pepper to taste
500 ml (2 cups) button mushrooms, sliced
1 green pepper, seeded and sliced
1 large onion, finely chopped
1–2 cloves garlic, finely chopped
4 chicken thighs, skinned and deboned,
cooked and cut into strips

To make the white sauce, mix together the flour, milk, milk powder and stock powders in a saucepan. Heat until very thick, stirring all the time. Season well.

In a separate saucepan, sauté the mushrooms, green pepper, onion and garlic until soft and juice has formed. Add the chicken.

Stir this mixture into the white sauce. Serve with rice or pasta. **Serves 4–6**

Chicken Tandoori

pepper chicken with mustard sauce

4 chicken breasts, skinned and deboned
10 ml (2 teaspoons) crushed black peppercorns
2 ml (¼ teaspoon) salt
5 ml (1 teaspoon) olive oil
60 ml (¼ cup) dry white wine or water
4 spring onions, chopped
5 ml (1 teaspoon) chicken stock powder
dissolved in 250 ml (1 cup) hot water
60 ml (¼ cup) fat-free or low-fat plain yoghurt
mixed with 10 ml (2 teaspoons) cornflour
10 ml (2 teaspoons) Dijon mustard, or to taste
snipped fresh chives to garnish (optional)

Preheat the oven to 220 °C (425 °F). Lightly grease a shallow baking dish.

Press the peppercorns into the chicken breasts and sprinkle with salt and olive oil. Bake for 15–20 minutes, or until juices run clear when the chicken is pricked with a fork.

In a small saucepan, boil the wine or water and spring onions, uncovered, until the wine has reduced to 30 ml (2 tablespoons). Add the stock and boil for about 2 minutes, or until the liquid has reduced to 250 ml (1 cup). Reduce heat and add the yoghurt mixture. Whisk for 1 minute, then stir in the mustard.

Slice the breasts diagonally, arrange on a platter and spoon over the sauce. Garnish with chives. Serve with boiled potatoes. **Serves 4–6**

chicken with herb sauce

4–6 chicken breasts, skinned and deboned
chicken stock to cover or 1 chicken stock cube
dissolved in 750 ml (3 cups) hot water
celery leaves, chopped
1 onion, chopped
black peppercorns
1 bay leaf

herb sauce
180 ml (¾ cup) Bulgarian yoghurt
or fat-free plain yoghurt
180 ml (¾ cup) buttermilk
15 ml (1 tablespoon) sour cream and
chives oil-free salad dressing
15 ml (1 tablespoon) lemon juice
2 cloves garlic, crushed
1 bunch chives, dill or basil, chopped
½ bunch parsley, chopped
salt and freshly ground black pepper to taste

Grease a heavy-based pan with non-stick spray. Arrange the breasts in the pan, and pour over the stock. Add the celery leaves, onion, peppercorns and bay leaf. Cover, bring to the boil, then reduce heat and simmer for about 10 minutes, or until just cooked through.

Remove from heat and leave the chicken to cool in the broth. Once cooled, remove the chicken and refrigerate.

Combine all the sauce ingredients. Slice the breasts, spoon over the sauce and garnish with lemon wedges, watercress and salad leaves. Serves 4

chicken and tomato bake

2–4 chicken breasts, skinned,
deboned and cut into strips
1 clove garlic, crushed
60 ml (¼ cup) white or red wine, or water
1 x 410 g can tomato and onion mix
5 ml (1 teaspoon) chopped fresh parsley
250 ml (1 cup) button mushrooms, sliced
4 courgettes (baby marrows), sliced
1 green pepper, seeded and sliced

Preheat the oven to 180 °C (350 °F).

Grease a casserole dish with non–stick spray and place the chicken in the dish. Mix together the remaining ingredients and spoon over the chicken. Bake uncovered for 25 minutes, or until cooked. **Serves 2–4**

spicy chicken

1 onion, chopped
1 green pepper, seeded and finely chopped
1 clove garlic, crushed
1 curry leaf
1 fresh chilli, seeded and finely chopped
(optional)
400 g chicken breasts, skinned, deboned and cubed
30–60 ml (2–4 tablespoons) curry powder
1 chicken stock cube dissolved
in 500 ml (2 cups) hot water

Grease a heavy-based pan with non-stick spray and heat.

Dry-fry the onion, green pepper, garlic, curry leaf and chilli (if using). Stir in the chicken pieces. Add the curry powder and stock, and bring to the boil. Reduce heat and simmer until cooked.

Serve with rice and salad. **Serves 4**

chicken provençale

sauce
1 onion, finely chopped
4 cloves garlic, crushed
1 x 410 g can whole peeled tomatoes,
chopped, juice reserved
7 ml (1¼ teaspoons) sugar
10 ml (2 teaspoons) mustard powder
30 ml (2 tablespoons) white wine
10 ml (2 teaspoons) dried tarragon or basil

4 chicken breasts, skinned and deboned
salt and freshly ground black pepper to taste
5 ml (1 teaspoon) mustard seeds

Grease a heavy-based pan with non-stick spray and dry-fry the onion and garlic.

Add the tomatoes, sugar, 5 ml (1 teaspoon) mustard powder, wine and tarragon or basil. Bring to the boil, then reduce heat.

Meanwhile, season the chicken with salt, pepper and 5 ml (1 teaspoon) mustard powder, and set aside.

Dry-fry the mustard seeds over a gentle heat and, when they begin to pop, add the chicken. Cook for 3–4 minutes on each side.

Season the sauce to taste, and spoon over the chicken breasts. **Serves 4**

french-style casserole

marinade
1 clove garlic, crushed
125 ml (½ cup) red wine vinegar
125 ml (½ cup) red wine
15 ml (1 tablespoon) soy sauce
salt and freshly ground black pepper to taste

4 chicken breasts (about 175 g each), skinned
60 ml (¼ cup) brandy
250 ml (1 cup) pickling onions, peeled
2–4 carrots, peeled and sliced
1–2 chicken stock cubes dissolved
in 1 litre (4 cups) hot water
250 ml (1 cup) button mushrooms, chopped
salt and freshly ground black pepper to taste
chopped fresh parsley to garnish

Combine all the marinade ingredients. Place the chicken in a large shallow bowl and cover with marinade. Set aside in a cool place for at least 3 hours.

Preheat the oven to 220 °C (425 °F).

Remove the chicken from the marinade and briefly brown under the grill. Transfer the chicken to a casserole dish.

Pour the brandy over the chicken and carefully ignite. When the flames die down, add the onions, carrots and stock. Cover, place in the oven and cook for 15 minutes.

Add the mushrooms and seasoning, and cook for a further 10 minutes, or until the chicken is tender and juices run clear when pierced in the thickest part.

Meanwhile, pour the marinade into a saucepan and boil rapidly, uncovered, until reduced by half. Stir the sauce into the casserole and garnish with chopped parsley.

Serve with steamed beans and salad. **Serves 4–6**

poached chicken

500 ml (2 cups) water
60 ml (¼ cup) dry white wine or water
1 chicken stock cube
1 bay leaf
2 chicken breasts (about 175 g each), skinned

Combine the water, wine, stock cube and bay leaf in a shallow pan. Add the chicken and, if necessary, add extra water to barely cover the chicken. Bring to the boil, then reduce heat and simmer, uncovered, for 10 minutes, or until the chicken is tender. Do not over-cook or the chicken will be dry and tough.

Remove the chicken from the stock, and serve with a sauce of your choice. **Serves 2**

Serving suggestion: Cold poached chicken served with a salad is an ideal light lunch or dinner.

French-style Casserole

meat

lamb with vinaigrette sauce

4 lamb chops or 8 lamb cutlets, fat removed
4 ml (¾ teaspoon) mustard powder
freshly ground black pepper

vinaigrette sauce
2 cloves garlic, crushed
30 ml (2 tablespoons) chopped fresh rosemary
5 ml (1 teaspoon) whole grain mustard
4 ml (¾ teaspoon) brown sugar
60 ml (¼ cup) Balsamic or red wine vinegar
salt and freshly ground black pepper to taste

Preheat the grill.
Season the chops with mustard powder and pepper.
Place in a greased casserole dish and grill until cooked.
To make the sauce, place all the ingredients in a small
saucepan, bring to the boil and simmer for 2 minutes.
Spoon the sauce over the chops and serve. **Serves 4**

Note: For a mint-flavoured vinaigrette sauce
use mint instead of rosemary.

shepherd's pie

450 g lean minced beef
250–500 ml (1–2 cups) water
1 large onion, finely chopped
5 ml (1 teaspoon) dried mixed herbs
salt and freshly ground black pepper to taste
5 ml (1 teaspoon) Marmite
15–20 ml (3–4 teaspoons) gravy powder
4 potatoes, peeled

Preheat the oven to 160 °C (325 °F).

Boil the mince and water in a saucepan for about 5 minutes, then drain, reserving the liquid. Place the mince in a covered container, and set aside until required.

Place the reserved liquid in the refrigerator. This will cause fat to rise to the top and enable you to remove it.

Return the skimmed liquid to the saucepan. Add the mince, onion, herbs, seasoning and Marmite.

Mix the gravy powder with a little water, and add to the meat mixture.

Bring to the boil, stirring; reduce heat and simmer for 10 minutes.

In a separate saucepan, boil the potatoes until soft. Drain some of the water, and mash. Add water, if necessary, for a smoother texture.

Place the mince in an ovenproof dish and cover with mashed potatoes. Place in the oven to brown.

Serve with vegetables. **Serves 4**

spaghetti bolognese

450 g lean minced beef
salt and freshly ground black pepper to taste
1 large onion, chopped
2 cloves garlic, crushed
1 carrot, peeled and finely grated
1 stick celery, finely sliced
1 x 410 g can chopped tomatoes
125 ml (½ cup) tomato purée
3 ml (½ teaspoon) dried origanum
1 beef stock cube
500 g spaghetti

Heat a non-stick pan and sprinkle with black pepper. Dry-fry mince until it changes colour.

Drain the mince and set aside. Wipe out the pan with kitchen paper and return to heat.

Add the onion, garlic, carrot and celery and cook until soft. Add the mince, tomatoes, purée, origanum, stock cube and seasoning and mix. Cook until the meat is done.

Prepare the spaghetti as per instructions on the packet and drain. Add the meat mixture to the cooked spaghetti and serve. **Serves 4**

Shepherd's Pie

easy lamb and tomato curry

1 clove garlic, finely chopped
1 small onion, finely sliced
15 ml (1 tablespoon) curry powder
1 medium tomato, peeled and chopped
60 ml (¼ cup) water
4 lamb chops, deboned and fat removed
1 small apple, peeled, cored and chopped
15 ml (1 tablespoon) sultanas

Heat a non-stick pan and dry-fry the garlic, onion and curry powder, stirring constantly, for about 3 minutes, or until onion is soft.

Add tomato and water and stir constantly for about 1 minute.

Add the meat to the pan and stir constantly over high heat until the meat is well coated with the curry mixture.

Bring to the boil; reduce heat and simmer, covered, for 30 minutes, or until the lamb is tender.

Stir in the apple and sultanas. Simmer, covered, for a further 5 minutes, or until apple is tender.

Serve with saffron rice (add saffron to the water while the rice is boiling). **Serves 2**

Note: Curry can be prepared up to 2 days ahead of time, but must be kept in the refrigerator. It can also be frozen for up to 2 months.

patties with creamy dill sauce

400 g lean minced beef
45 ml (3 tablespoons) skim (fat-free) milk
1 large egg white
30 ml (2 tablespoons) dried breadcrumbs
45 ml (3 tablespoons) chopped fresh dill
or 5 ml (1 teaspoon) dried dill
3 ml (½ teaspoon) mustard powder
2 ml (¼ teaspoon) salt
2 ml (¼ teaspoon) freshly ground black pepper
1 medium onion, finely chopped
1 clove garlic, crushed
45 ml (3 tablespoons) cake flour
½ stock cube dissolved in 125 ml
(½ cup) hot water
60 ml (¼ cup) fat-free or low-fat plain yoghurt

Preheat the oven to 180 °C (350 °F).

In a medium-sized bowl, combine the mince, milk, egg white, breadcrumbs, half the dill, the mustard powder, salt, pepper, onion and garlic.

Wet your hands and shape the mince mixture into 24 patties, each about 4 cm in diameter.

Roll the patties in flour and shake off the excess. Place in a casserole dish and bake for 20–30 minutes, or until golden brown on all sides.

In a saucepan, add the stock, bring to the boil and simmer for 5 minutes. Remove from heat and stir in the yoghurt and remaining dill. **Serves 4**

spicy pot roast

1.25 kg topside beef, trimmed of fat
3 ml (½ teaspoon) cayenne pepper, or to taste
salt and freshly ground black pepper to taste
10 ml (2 teaspoons) olive oil or non-stick spray
1 medium onion, coarsely chopped
1 stick celery, coarsely chopped
1 large green pepper, seeded and coarsely chopped
2 cloves garlic, crushed
250 ml (1 cup) button mushrooms, halved
30–60 ml (2–4 tablespoons) cornflour
1 x 410 g can chopped tomatoes
1 x 410 g can tomato juice
1 cube beef stock dissolved in
250 ml (1 cup) hot water
3 ml (½ teaspoon) dried thyme
3 ml (½ teaspoon) dried basil
1 bay leaf
3 ml (½ teaspoon) cloves (optional)

Rub the meat with the cayenne pepper, salt and black pepper.

Heat the olive oil over moderate heat in a saucepan or use non-stick spray.

Add the meat, turning for 5 minutes or until brown, then transfer to a plate.

Add the onion, celery, green pepper, garlic and mushrooms to the saucepan, and stir until golden.

Add the cornflour and cook over low heat for 2 minutes, stirring.

Add the tomatoes, tomato juice, stock, thyme, basil, bay leaf and cloves, stirring constantly. Add the meat. Bring the liquid to the boil, reduce heat and simmer for 2–3 hours, or until the meat is tender.

Skim any fat from the surface of the cooking liquid and remove the bay leaf before serving.

Serve with rice, potatoes or pasta. **Serves 8**

lemon-tarragon veal

750 g veal, trimmed of fat and
cut into 2.5 cm cubes
125 ml (½ cup) dry white wine
125 ml (½ cup) lemon juice
10 ml (2 teaspoons) chopped fresh tarragon
or 5 ml (1 teaspoon) dried
1 chicken stock cube dissolved in
165 ml (⅔ cup) hot water
salt and freshly ground black pepper to taste
8 ml (1½ teaspoons) cornflour (optional)

Preheat the oven to 150 ℃ (300 ℉).

Place the veal in a casserole dish and add all the remaining ingredients except the cornflour, if using.

Bake for about 2 hours, or until the veal is tender.

If you prefer a thicker sauce, mix the cornflour with a little water to form a paste and stir into the casserole. Heat gently, stirring, for about 1 minute ,or until thickened.

Skim any fat from the surface of the cooking liquid before serving. **Serves 4**

sirloin steaks with tomato-garlic sauce

4 sirloin steaks, trimmed of fat and
beaten with a mallet until thin
6–8 large tomatoes, skinned and chopped
3 cloves garlic, crushed
15 ml (1 tablespoon) chopped fresh basil
or 5 ml (1 teaspoon) dried basil
salt and freshly ground black pepper to taste
fresh basil or parsley sprigs to garnish

Preheat the grill. Grill the steaks for 8–10 minutes, or until cooked to your liking, turning once.

Place the tomatoes, garlic, basil and seasoning in a saucepan, and simmer until tomatoes are soft.

Transfer the steaks to a heated serving dish and spoon over the sauce. Garnish with sprigs of basil. Serves 4

veal paprika

4 veal escalopes (about 175 g each)
15 ml (1 tablespoon) lemon juice
60 ml (¼ cup) tomato purée
15 ml (1 tablespoon) paprika
375 ml (1½ cups) fat-free
or low-fat plain yoghurt
salt and freshly ground black pepper to taste
twist of lemon to garnish

Preheat the grill. Grill the veal for 5 minutes on each side, brushing frequently with lemon juice.

In a saucepan, mix together the tomato purée, paprika, yoghurt and remaining lemon juice. Heat gently. Season to taste.

Transfer the veal to a heated serving dish and spoon over the sauce.

Garnish with a twist of lemon and serve with steamed cauliflower. Serves 4

Note: This easy paprika sauce is also ideal for serving with pork chops.

Sirloin Steaks with Tomato-garlic Sauce

pasta

pasta with sundried tomatoes

500 g tagliatelle, fettucine, spaghetti or pasta shells
250 ml (1 cup) grated butternut
1 clove garlic, crushed
2 spring onions, finely chopped
1 green pepper, seeded and finely chopped
250 ml (1 cup) sundried tomatoes
3 ml (½ teaspoon) dried thyme
15 ml (1 tablespoon) olive oil
salt and freshly ground black pepper to taste

Cook the pasta with the butternut, garlic, spring onions and green pepper for the cooking time stipulated on the pasta packet. Drain and transfer to a serving dish. Add the remaining ingredients, mix well and serve. **Serves 4–6**

pasta with origanum sauce

125 ml (½ cup) water
2 cloves garlic, crushed
5 ml (1 teaspoon) chilli powder
4 ripe tomatoes, skinned, or 1 x 410 g can
peeled tomatoes, cut into strips
salt and freshly ground black pepper to taste
45 ml (3 tablespoons) finely chopped
fresh origanum or 15 ml (1 tablespoon)
dried origanum
500 g tagliatelle, fettucine, spaghetti
or pasta shells, cooked

Heat a saucepan over high heat and add the water. When the water starts to simmer, add the garlic and chilli powder, stirring quickly. Remove from heat and add the tomato strips, seasoning and origanum.

Serve over cooked pasta. **Serves 4**

mushroom pasta

juice of 2–4 lemons
5 ml (1 teaspoon) chopped fresh basil
5 ml (1 teaspoon) chopped fresh parsley
1 clove garlic, crushed (optional)
freshly ground black pepper to taste
500 ml (2 cups) button mushrooms, finely sliced
250 g tagliatelle, fettucine, spaghetti
or pasta shells

In a large bowl, mix together the lemon juice, herbs, garlic (if using) and seasoning. Add the mushrooms to the lemon juice mixture, then cover the bowl with cling film and leave to stand in a cool place for 1 hour.

In the meantime, prepare the pasta according to the instructions on the packet, drain and add to the lemon mixture. This pasta can be served hot or cold. **Serves 4**

Note: A mixture of button mushrooms, brown mushrooms and oyster mushrooms can be used.

For a different flavour, use the Orange and Lemon Vinaigrette (see page 38) as a marinade for the mushrooms.

tomato and basil pasta

1 onion, finely chopped
6–8 large tomatoes, skinned,
seeded and chopped
30 ml (2 tablespoons) tomato purée
juice and grated rind of 1 orange
125 ml (½ cup) red wine
1 vegetable stock cube dissolved in
125 ml (½ cup) hot water
2 cloves garlic, crushed
30 ml (2 tablespoons) coarsely chopped
fresh basil
1 fresh chilli, seeded and finely chopped
(optional)
salt and freshly ground black pepper to taste
400 g tagliatelle, fettucine, spaghetti
or pasta shells

In a large non-stick pan, fry the onion, tomatoes and purée over a low heat, stirring continuously.

Add the remaining ingredients, except the pasta, and boil until the sauce has reduced and thickened and the vegetables are soft.

Prepare the pasta, drain and add to the sauce.

Serves 4–6

macaroni with butternut and mushrooms

125 ml (½ cup) grated butternut
2 spring onions, finely chopped
30 ml (2 tablespoons) fat-free milk powder
dissolved in 1 litre (4 cups) skim (fat-free) milk
3 ml (½ teaspoon) mustard powder
5 ml (1 teaspoon) vegetable stock powder
5 ml (1 teaspoon) soy sauce
3 ml (½ teaspoon) dried dill
3 ml (½ teaspoon) dried basil
3 ml (½ teaspoon) dried origanum
30 ml (2 tablespoons) cornflour or cake flour
500 g macaroni
500 ml (2 cups) button mushrooms, halved
5 ml (1 teaspoon) paprika

Preheat the oven to 180 °C (350 °F).

Dry-fry the butternut with the spring onions until well cooked. Place in a blender with a little milk and blend to form a smooth paste.

Pour the butternut mixture into a saucepan and add the mustard powder, stock powder, soy sauce, herbs and remaining milk. Heat through.

Make a paste with the flour and a little milk. Add to the sauce to thicken, and stir well.

Cook the pasta and drain. Add the sauce and mushrooms to the pasta, mix together, then empty it into a casserole dish.

Sprinkle with paprika and bake for 20–25 minutes.

Serves 4–6

vegetables

steam-fried vegetables

1 bunch spring onions, chopped
2–6 cloves garlic, finely chopped
30–120 ml (2–8 tablespoons) soy sauce
or tamari sauce
handful carrots, sliced into thin strips (julienne)
1 green pepper, seeded and thinly sliced
1 red pepper, seeded and thinly sliced
250–500 ml (1–2 cups) button mushrooms, halved
handful green beans and/or sugar snap peas (mangetout)
large handful bean sprouts
large handful bamboo shoots
15–30 ml (1–2 tablespoons) grated fresh ginger (optional)
1–2 tomatoes, skinned and chopped (optional)
handful chopped fresh coriander (optional)

Steam-fry the spring onions, garlic and soy sauce in a wok.
Add a little water and the remaining vegetables, and simmer
until the vegetables are cooked but still crunchy. **Serves 4–6**

aubergines and rice

2 small aubergines (brinjals)
1 onion, finely chopped
1 clove garlic, crushed
2 large tomatoes, skinned, seeded and chopped
180 ml (¾ cup) rice, cooked
10 ml (2 teaspoons) chopped fresh marjoram
pinch of ground cinnamon
salt and freshly ground black pepper to taste
finely chopped fresh parsley to garnish

Preheat the oven to 180 °C (350 °F).

Wrap the aubergines in aluminium foil and bake for 20 minutes to soften. Leave to cool.

Cut the aubergines in half and carefully scoop out the pulp, leaving enough to make a thick shell.

Dry-fry the onion and garlic until soft.

Chop the aubergine pulp and stir it into the onion mixture. Cover and cook for 5 minutes.

Add the tomatoes, rice, marjoram, cinnamon and seasoning.

Carefully pile the rice filling back into the aubergine shells and arrange on a baking sheet.

Cover with foil and bake for 20 minutes.

Serve hot, garnished with parsley. **Serves 4**

sweet peppers

2 cloves garlic, crushed
2 shallots, finely chopped
30 ml (2 tablespoons) capers
180 ml (¾ cup) button mushrooms, sliced
30 ml (2 tablespoons) cake flour
1 vegetable stock cube dissolved in
300 ml (1¼ cups) hot water
20 ml (4 teaspoons) prepared mustard
10 ml (2 teaspoons) Worcestershire sauce
30 ml (2 tablespoons) white wine
10 ml (2 teaspoons) lemon juice
pinch each of dried thyme and rosemary
8 baby corn on the cob
1 green pepper, seeded and finely sliced
1 red pepper, seeded and finely sliced
1 yellow pepper, seeded and finely sliced
4 tomatoes, skinned, seeded and
cut into thin strips
salt and freshly ground black pepper to taste

Dry-fry the garlic, shallots, capers and mushrooms. Sprinkle over flour and sauté until soft.

Pour over stock and stir well, then add the mustard, Worcestershire sauce, wine, lemon juice, thyme and rosemary.

Add the corn, peppers, tomatoes and seasoning and simmer for 5 minutes.

Serve with rice or baked potatoes. **Serves 2–4**

Aubergines and Rice

stuffed brown mushrooms

8 large brown mushrooms,
wiped and stalks removed
4–6 cloves garlic, finely chopped
15 ml (1 tablespoon) finely chopped fresh parsley
1 small onion or spring onion, chopped
½ green pepper, seeded and finely sliced
½ red pepper, seeded and finely sliced
½ yellow pepper, seeded and finely sliced
freshly ground coarse sea salt to taste

Preheat the grill.

Grease a baking sheet with non-stick spray. Place the upturned mushrooms on the sheet.

Mix the garlic, parsley and onion or spring onion together, and spoon 3 ml (½ teaspoon) of the mixture over each mushroom. Top with green, red and yellow pepper slices, and season.

Grill for 4–10 minutes, until mushrooms are soft. Serves 4–6

vegetable curry

1 onion, finely chopped
1 stick celery, sliced
10 ml (2 teaspoons) curry powder
10 ml (2 teaspoons) vegetable stock powder
375 ml (1½ cups) water
1 turnip, peeled and chopped
3 carrots, peeled and sliced
3 potatoes, peeled and chopped
salt and freshly ground black pepper to taste

Dry-fry the onion, celery and curry powder. Add the vegetable stock powder.

Add the remaining ingredients, bring to the boil and simmer for 20–30 minutes.

For a thicker sauce, remove the potatoes, blend and stir back into the curry. Serves 2–4

baked stuffed onions

4 large onions, peeled
enough water to cover onions
250–500 ml (1–2 cups) chopped
button mushrooms
1 clove garlic, crushed
4 spring onions, finely chopped
15 ml (1 tablespoon) soy sauce
3 ml (½ teaspoon) dried thyme
salt and freshly ground black pepper to taste

Preheat the oven to 180 °C (350 °F).

Place the onions in a saucepan, cover with water, and bring to the boil. Simmer for 20 minutes until the onions are tender. Slice off the tops of the onions and remove the centres with a teaspoon, leaving a shell for the filling.

Dry-fry the mushrooms, garlic, spring onions and onion centres. Add the soy sauce, thyme and seasoning.

Fill the onion shells with the stuffing and place side by side in a casserole dish. Pour a little water into the dish, cover, and bake for 30–45 minutes, or until the onions are golden. Serves 4

creamed spinach

1 large packet or bunch fresh spinach,
large, tough veins removed
5 ml (1 teaspoon) salt
1 large onion, chopped
375 ml (1½ cups) skim (fat-free) milk
45 ml (3 tablespoons) fat-free milk powder
30–45 ml (2–3 tablespoons) cornflour
salt and freshly ground black pepper to taste
5 ml (1 teaspoon) vegetable stock powder
1 clove garlic, crushed

Boil the spinach in a little water, together with the salt and onion, until soft. When cooked, drain very well and chop finely.

Heat 375 ml (1½ cups) milk in a saucepan over gentle heat. Mix a little milk with the milk powder and cornflour to form a paste.

When the milk is warm (not boiling), stir in the paste. When thickened, add the seasoning, stock powder and garlic. Stir the white sauce into the chopped spinach and serve. **Serves 4**

steam-fried vegetables and protein

vegetables
1 bunch spring onions, chopped
2–6 cloves garlic, finely chopped
30–120 ml (2–8 tablespoons) soy sauce
or tamari sauce
handful carrots, sliced into thin strips (julienned)
1 green pepper, seeded and thinly sliced
1 red pepper, seeded and thinly sliced
250–500 ml (1–2 cups)
button mushrooms, halved
handful green beans and/or sugar snap peas
(mangetout)
large handful bean sprouts
large handful bamboo shoots
15–30 ml (1–2 tablespoons) grated fresh ginger
(optional)
1–2 tomatoes, skinned and chopped (optional)
handful chopped fresh coriander (optional)

protein
(select one of the following per recipe)
250 ml (1 cup) cubed chicken
250 ml (1 cup) cubed filleted fish
375 ml (1½ cups) cubed tempeh*
250 ml (1 cup) cubed tofu

Steam-fry the spring onions, garlic and soy sauce in a wok.

Add the chicken or fish and steam-fry until cooked. Add a little water and the remaining vegetables, and simmer until the vegetables are cooked but still crunchy.

If using tempeh or tofu, add the vegetables to the wok first. **Serves 4–6**

* Tempeh is a versatile soy product that has a meaty texture and is a delicious alternative to animal protein.

vegetable casserole

4 carrots, peeled and sliced
4 parsnips, sliced
2 large courgettes (baby marrows), sliced
2 turnips, peeled and sliced
1 red pepper, seeded and coarsely chopped
1 green pepper, seeded and coarsely chopped
1 yellow pepper, seeded and coarsely chopped
2 onions, sliced
2 large tomatoes, skinned, seeded and chopped
2 cubes vegetable or chicken stock dissolved
in 625 ml (2½ cups) hot water
1 bay leaf
15 ml (1 tablespoon) chopped fresh parsley
5 ml (1 teaspoon) chopped fresh thyme
5 ml (1 teaspoon) chopped fresh marjoram
5 ml (1 teaspoon) Worcestershire sauce
salt and freshly ground black pepper to taste

Place all the ingredients in a saucepan and bring to the boil.

Cover and cook gently for about 25 minutes.

This dish can be served on its own, or with grilled chicken. **Serves 4**

roast peppers and aubergine

60 ml (¼ cup) soy sauce
30 ml (2 tablespoons) white wine vinegar
4 cloves garlic, crushed
3 ml (½ teaspoon) ground ginger
3 ml (½ teaspoon) crushed red chilli
or black pepper
1 large aubergine (brinjal) (about 500 g), sliced
2 large red peppers (250 g each), seeded
and cut lengthways into 3 cm wide strips
2 large green peppers (250 g each), seeded
and cut lengthways into 3 cm wide strips
2 large yellow peppers (250 g each), seeded
and cut lengthways into 3 cm wide strips
30 ml (2 tablespoons) chopped fresh basil
30 ml (2 tablespoons) chopped fresh parsley

Preheat the grill and set the rack about 15 cm from the element.

Line a grilling pan with foil and lightly grease with non-stick spray.

In a small bowl, mix the soy sauce, vinegar, garlic, ginger and chilli or pepper together.

Brush the mixture over both sides of the aubergine and pepper slices and arrange them in the pan. Top with basil and parsley.

Grill for 4–6 minutes on each side, until golden brown. **Serves 4–6**

Vegetable Casserole and Sourdough Bread (p. 95)

potatoes with herbs and red wine

4 spring onions, finely chopped
5 medium potatoes, peeled and thinly sliced
1 vegetable stock cube
125 ml (½ cup) dry red wine or 125 ml (½ cup)
chicken stock mixed with 5 ml (1 teaspoon)
red wine vinegar
5 ml (1 teaspoon) dried thyme
5 ml (1 teaspoon) dried basil
5 ml (1 teaspoon) dried parsley
salt and freshly ground black pepper to taste
grated Parmesan cheese (optional)

Preheat the oven to 180 °C (350 °F).

Heat a non-stick pan. Add a little water and the spring onions and potatoes, and stir for 2 minutes.

Add the stock cube, wine or stock mixture, herbs and seasoning. Cook for 2–3 minutes, or until the liquid boils.

Spoon the potatoes and liquid into a lightly greased 20 cm square baking dish, and cover with aluminium foil. Bake for 1 hour.

Uncover and bake for about 15 minutes, until the potatoes are soft. Sprinkle with Parmesan and serve. **Serves 4**

french beans and peppers

500 ml (2 cups) French beans, topped and tailed
pinch of salt
1 large red pepper, seeded and chopped
8 ml (1½ teaspoons) chopped fresh basil
8 ml (1½ teaspoons) chopped fresh origanum
salt and freshly ground black pepper to taste

Cook the beans in boiling, salted water for 6–12 minutes, until tender. Drain and cut the beans in half.

Blanch the red pepper in boiling water for 1 minute, then drain.

Place the beans in a serving dish and add the red pepper. Sprinkle with herbs and season to taste. **Serves 4**

fat-free roast potatoes

4 medium potatoes, peeled and halved
1 vegetable stock cube
salt to taste

Preheat the oven to 180 °C (350 °F).

Place potatoes in a saucepan filled with cold water. Add the stock cube and boil for 5 minutes.

Drain the potatoes and pat dry with kitchen paper. Set aside until cool enough to handle. Cut potatoes in half again lengthways.

Place the potatoes on a non-stick baking sheet and sprinkle with salt. Bake for 55–60 minutes, turning occasionally during cooking so that the potatoes brown evenly. **Serves 4**

vegetable kebabs

2 medium onions, quartered
(cocktail onions can also be used)
1 large green pepper, seeded and
cut into bite-sized pieces
1 large red pepper, seeded and
cut into bite-sized pieces
1 large yellow pepper, seeded and
cut into bite-sized pieces
500 ml (2 cups) button mushrooms,
wiped but left whole
4 medium firm tomatoes, quartered
or 8–10 cherry tomatoes
8 bay leaves

Preheat the grill.

Soak two large or four small wooden skewers in water before use to prevent burning.

Thread bite-sized pieces of onion, green, red and yellow pepper, mushrooms and tomato alternately onto the skewers. Add a bay leaf at intervals for extra flavour.

Place the skewers under a moderate grill, or on the barbecue, turning from time to time to prevent burning.

Serve with brown rice. **Serves 2**

garlic mushrooms

½ vegetable stock cube dissolved in
300 ml (1¼ cups) hot water
3 cloves garlic, crushed
8–10 button mushrooms, wiped but left whole
salt and freshly ground black pepper to taste

Place the stock and garlic in a saucepan. Bring to the boil, reduce heat and simmer for 5 minutes on a gentle heat. Add the mushrooms and seasoning, cover with a lid and simmer for a further 5 minutes. **Serves 2**

ratatouille

250–500 ml (1–2 cups) courgettes
(baby marrows), sliced
2 aubergines (brinjals), sliced
1 green pepper, seeded and cut into strips
1 red pepper, seeded and cut into strips
1 yellow pepper, seeded and cut into strips
2 onions, sliced into rings
1 x 410 g can tomatoes
2 cloves garlic, crushed
2 bay leaves
salt and freshly ground black pepper to taste

Place all the ingredients in a large saucepan, bring to the boil and skim off any sediment. Cover and simmer for about 20 minutes, until the vegetables are tender.

If there is too much liquid remaining at the end of the cooking time, reduce by boiling it for a few minutes with the lid removed. **Serves 2**

desserts

baked pears

180 ml (¾ cup) canned cranberry sauce
60 ml (¼ cup) red wine
2 ml (¼ teaspoon) ground cinnamon
4 ripe pears, peeled, cored and halved
fresh mint to garnish (optional)

Mix together the cranberry sauce, wine and cinnamon. Place the pears in a saucepan and pour over sauce. Cover and gently simmer until the pears are tender. Place in a serving dish and spoon over sauce. Garnish with mint if desired. **Serves 4**

baked apples

4 apples, cored (pears can also be used)
60 ml (¼ cup) brown sugar or honey
15 raisins
180 ml (¾ cup) fat-free or low-fat plain yoghurt
ground cinnamon, nutmeg or mixed spice

Preheat the oven to 180 °C (350 °F).
Place apples on a plate and spoon sugar or honey into the core with the raisins.
Bake for 15–30 minutes, until apples are shrivelled.
Transfer the apples to a serving platter or individual bowls and pour the remaining melted sugar over them.
Pour a little yoghurt over each apple, and sprinkle with nutmeg, cinnamon or mixed spice. **Serves 4**

coffee sorbet

500 ml (2 cups) hot water
60 ml (¼ cup) skim (fat-free) milk powder
20 ml (4 teaspoons) instant coffee powder
2–3 drops vanilla essence
artificial sweetener to taste (optional)
2 egg whites
60 ml (¼ cup) fat-free or low-fat plain yoghurt
finely grated orange rind to garnish

Place the water in a bowl and stir in the milk powder, coffee, vanilla essence and sweetener (if using). Stir well to mix. Pour into a shallow, rigid container and place in the freezer for 1–2 hours, until the edges are frozen.

Whisk the egg whites until stiff. Beat the sorbet well, then fold in the egg whites and return to the freezer for 1 hour. Beat again and return the sorbet to the freezer for another hour.

Serve in chilled glasses; spoon 15 ml (1 tablespoon) yoghurt on top and sprinkle with finely grated orange rind. **Serves 4**

fruit kebabs

1 Granny Smith apple, cored and cubed
(do not peel)
1 Starking apple, cored and cubed (do not peel)
1 banana, sliced into bite-sized pieces
juice of 1 lemon
1 orange, peeled, pith removed and cut into
bite-sized pieces
6 black grapes, halved and pips removed
5 white grapes, halved and pips removed
250 ml (1 cup) fat-free or low-fat plain yoghurt
5 ml (1 teaspoon) honey

Fruit kebabs can be served fresh or baked. If baking, preheat the oven to 180 °C (350 °F).

Soak four wooden skewers in water before use to prevent burning. Thread the fruit pieces alternately onto the skewers and bake on a covered non-stick tray for 15–35 minutes, until golden.

If you prefer fresh kebabs, coat the apples and banana with a little lemon juice to prevent them from going brown. Thread the fruit pieces alternately onto the skewers. Blend the yoghurt with the honey and use as a dipping sauce. **Serves 2–4**

frozen yoghurt parfait

500 ml (2 cups) fresh strawberries,
raspberries or blueberries
45 ml (3 tablespoons) sugar
15 ml (1 tablespoon) lemon juice
5 ml (1 teaspoon) grated lemon rind
500 ml (2 cups) fat-free frozen vanilla yoghurt,
slightly softened

Blend half the berries with the sugar, lemon juice and lemon rind for 15 seconds, until smooth.

Transfer the mixture to a medium-sized bowl and stir in the remaining berries.

Layer the mixture with the frozen yoghurt in four tall glasses. Freeze for 45 minutes, until firm. **Serves 4**

basmati rice pudding

125 ml (½ cup) Basmati rice
625 ml (2½ cups) skim (fat-free) milk
85 ml (⅓ cup) castor sugar
3 cardamom or vanilla pods
1 bay leaf
ground cinnamon

Place the rice, milk, sugar, cardamom or vanilla pods and bay leaf in a heavy-based, non-stick saucepan. Bring to the boil, stirring constantly. Reduce heat and simmer. Cook for 30 minutes, stirring occasionally, until thick and the rice is soft.

If the milk starts to evaporate during cooking, add a little water and cook gently, until liquid has reduced. Cool, stirring occasionally. Remove the cardamom or vanilla pods and bay leaf.

Spoon into dishes and sprinkle with a little cinnamon. **Serves 3**

fat-free custard

60 ml (¼ cup) custard powder
60 ml (¼ cup) artificial sweetener or clear honey
500 ml (2 cups) skim (fat-free) milk

Mix the custard powder and sweetener or honey with 50 ml milk to form a smooth paste. Bring remaining milk to the boil. Remove from heat and add it to the paste. Return to heat and stir until thick. Serve with fresh, stewed or baked fruit. **Serves 2–4**

creamy whipped topping

3 ml (½ teaspoon) unflavoured gelatin powder
15 ml (1 tablespoon) water
250 ml (1 cup) fat-free or low-fat smooth cottage cheese
15 ml (1 tablespoon) honey
15 ml (1 tablespoon) brown sugar
2 ml (¼ teaspoon) vanilla essence

In a small heatproof bowl, sprinkle the gelatin over the water and soften for 5 minutes.

Meanwhile, in a saucepan, bring about 1 cm depth of water to a simmer over low heat. Place the bowl in the simmering water and stir until the gelatin has dissolved.

Blend the cottage cheese, honey, sugar and vanilla essence for 1 minute until creamy. Add the gelatin and blend for 30 seconds until smooth. Spoon into a small bowl, cover and chill for 2 hours or until thickened, stirring occasionally. Serve over fresh berries or dessert. **Makes 250 ml (1 cup)**

strawberry delight

2 x 80 g packets strawberry jelly to
make 500 ml (2 cups)
500–1000 ml (2–4 cups) fresh strawberries
125 ml (½ cup) skim (fat–free) milk powder
fresh mint leaves and strawberries to garnish

Prepare the jelly as per the instructions on the packet. Blend the strawberries and mix into the warm jelly.

Add the milk powder and whip with an electric mixer until light and fluffy.

Pour into a mould and leave in the refrigerator overnight to set. Garnish with mint leaves and fresh strawberries. **Serves 4–6**

Note: This dessert can also be made with peaches and peach jelly.

fruit trifle

4 ginger biscuits, crushed
60 ml (¼ cup) medium sherry
250 ml (1 cup) canned fruit cocktail, drained
180 ml (¾ cup) fat-free custard (see page 89)

Press crushed biscuits into the bottom of a small airtight container and sprinkle with half the sherry.

Add the remaining sherry to the fruit cocktail, then spoon the mixture over the biscuit base. Top with custard. Seal and refrigerate. **Serves 2**

curried fruit salad

1 x 820 g can fruit cocktail, drained
85 ml (⅓ cup) brown sugar or honey
7 ml (1¼ teaspoons) medium curry powder
pinch of ground cinnamon
pinch of ground cloves

Preheat the oven to 190 °C (375 °F).

Grease a shallow ovenproof dish with non-stick spray. Spoon the fruit into the dish.

Mix the sugar or honey, curry powder, cinnamon and cloves together, and sprinkle over the fruit.

Bake the fruit salad for 20 minutes, and serve hot with fat-free custard (see page 89) or creamy whipped topping (see page 89). **Serves 6**

Strawberry Delight

breads & muffins

raisin bran muffins

750 ml (3 cups) nutty wheat flour, sifted
375 ml (1½ cups) oats or wheat bran
10 ml (2 teaspoons) baking powder (optional)
5 ml (1 teaspoon) ground cinnamon
3 ml (½ teaspoon) grated nutmeg
3 ml (½ teaspoon) ground coriander
750 ml (3 cups) chopped apple
250 ml (1 cup) raisins
125 ml (½ cup) pear or apple juice mixed
with 250 ml (1 cup) water

Preheat the oven to 170 °C (340 °F).
Mix all the dry ingredients together in a large bowl.
Add the fruit to the mixture, then add the
fruit juice and water. Mix well.
Spoon the mixture into non-stick muffin trays lightly
greased with non-stick spray and bake for
20–30 minutes. **Makes 12–24 muffins**

Note: The raisins can be substituted with either
sultanas, nuts or mixed dried fruit.

banana bread

250 ml (1 cup) dark brown sugar
180 ml (¾ cup) apple sauce
3 large ripe bananas, mashed
4 egg whites
500 ml (2 cups) cake flour
pinch of salt
5 ml (1 teaspoon) bicarbonate of soda
60 ml (¼ cup) water
8 ml (1½ teaspoons) baking powder

Preheat the oven to 180 °C (350 °F).

Cream the sugar and apple sauce until smooth. Stir in the mashed bananas and mix thoroughly. Beat in the egg whites one at a time.

Sift the flour and salt into the mixture and mix well. Dissolve the bicarbonate of soda in the water, and combine into the mixture. Stir in the baking powder.

Pour the batter into a greased loaf tin and bake for 45 minutes.

Allow to cool for 10 minutes, then turn out onto rack and leave to cool completely. **Makes 1 loaf**

quick bread

7½ cups nutty wheat flour
45 ml (3 tablespoons) brown sugar
10 ml (2 teaspoons) bicarbonate of soda
10 ml (2 teaspoons) salt
1 litre (4 cups) buttermilk
2 ml (¼ teaspoon) vanilla essence

Preheat the oven to 180 °C (350 °F).

Mix all dry ingredients together in a large bowl.

Pour in the buttermilk and vanilla essence, and mix well.

Divide the dough between 2 non-stick bread tins greased with non-stick spray. Bake for 1 hour. **Makes 2 loaves**

Note: To make savoury loaves add thinly sliced onion, sundried tomatoes and green peppers when mixing in the buttermilk.

raisin bread

500 ml (2 cups) self-raising flour
15 ml (1 tablespoon) baking powder
5 ml (1 teaspoon) salt
180 ml (¾ cup) seedless raisins
125 ml (½ cup) brown sugar
500 ml (2 cups) warm water

Preheat the oven to 180 °C (350 °F). Grease a loaf tin with non-stick spray.

Sift together the flour, baking powder and salt. Add the raisins and sugar and mix. Add the water, and mix to form a soft dough.

Spoon the dough into the loaf tin and bake for 1¼ hours until cooked and light brown. Turn out onto a wire rack and leave to cool. **Makes 1 loaf**

sourdough bread

3 medium potatoes, peeled and coarsely grated
250 ml (1 cup) lukewarm water
30 ml (2 tablespoons) salt
60 ml (¼ cup) sugar
1 x 10 g packet instant yeast
250 ml (1 cup) cake flour

Preheat the oven to 200 °C (400 °F).

Mix the potatoes, water, salt, sugar and yeast together in a large bowl.

Sprinkle the flour over the mixture and leave in a warm place until foamy.

Use 250 ml (1 cup) of the mixture to make one loaf of bread. Bake for 35–45 minutes.

A small ovenproof bowl of water can also be placed in the oven with the bread for extra moisture. **Makes 3 loaves**

Note: The remaining dough can be kept in the refrigerator, covered with cling film, for later use. The container should only be filled halfway to allow for fermentation.

buttermilk bread with dried fruit

500 ml (2 cups) mixed dried fruit
625 ml (2½ cups) self-raising flour
250 ml (1 cup) brown sugar
5 ml (1 teaspoon) salt
750 ml (3 cups) buttermilk

Preheat the oven to 190 °C (375 °F). Grease two loaf tins with non-stick spray.

Remove pips from the prunes, then chop the mixed fruit until fine. Mix with the flour, sugar and salt. Add the buttermilk and combine well.

Divide the dough between two loaf tins and spread evenly.

Bake for about 1 hour until done. Turn out onto a wire rack and leave to cool. **Makes 2 loaves**

index